T0243597

BLACK SHEEP

BLACk
SHEEP

the Quest to
Be Human in an
Inhuman Time

Peter Eagle Sims

Printed in the United States of America 10 9 8 7 6 5 4 3 2 1

Distributed by Publishers Group West

Book design and production by Domini Dragoone

Library of Congress Control Number: 2023939711
ISBN (hardcover): 978-1-939714-25-1
ISBN (ebook): 978-1-939714-27-5

Published in the United States of America by Silicon Guild, an imprint of Missionday. Bulk purchase discounts, special editions, and customized excerpts are available direct from the publisher. For information about books for educational, business, or promotional purposes, or any other requests, please email: publisher@missionday.com

For Riley

"Born originals,

how comes it to pass

that we die copies?"

— EDWARD YOUNG,
PLAYWRIGHT AND POET

CONTENTS

CHAPTER ONE

THE
CAN'T FAIL
CAFE

The night the whole Black Sheep idea was born came out of nowhere, and not a moment too soon. It was August 4th, 2011. Back then, the only way I could get into Pixar Animation Studios was as a guest to see their in-house improv group perform. The Improvibles, as they called themselves, put on a performance after work once every month or two in one of the large Pixar screening theaters. I say "not a moment too soon" because I had nearly given up hope of finding an authentic path in life, or even living on several occasions. After years of seeking, I had surrendered. I wasn't going to be anything in life but Peter Sims, and I had accepted that. If I wasn't going to starve, anything else was gravy.

If you want to have an original life, feeling like you have absolutely nothing to lose may be the best starting point. Now, not all who wander are lost. But some who wander are really, *badly, completely* lost.

I ended up wandering for several years. I wanted to get away from the bullshit I had witnessed inside the capital markets as well as seeing the power structure up close. I felt so lost that when I drove and held the steering wheel, I sometimes didn't feel completely in my own body or fingers. At dinners or parties with new acquaintances, I didn't know how to introduce myself, which is such a vulnerable and raw place. My fiancé's family struggled to understand what was wrong with me, especially her grandmother, who seemed to think I was a lost cause professionally. She got her wish when we ended the engagement as our paths began to diverge. For several years, people often didn't return my phone calls. I interviewed unsuccessfully for a handful of jobs and wasn't hired, probably because I seemed so nervous or unsure of myself.

At one point, after about a year of meandering, my dad took me to lunch at an old Italian joint in San Francisco. He asked if I was sure I didn't want to go back into venture capital. "You could be the next Marty Mannion!" he enthused, referencing the respected, charismatic partner I had worked for at Summit Partners. As flattering and well-intended as Dad's suggestion was, as he spoke, stress engulfed my head. Over plates of pasta and grilled fish, I searched for words to explain that I was navigating a different path. Dad, always the lawyer-turned-judge, shared what I already knew: his career path had been much more linear. It was hard, he kindly put it, for him to relate.

"Are you sure you know what you're doing?" he asked towards the end of lunch.

"Yes; I know what I'm doing," I replied resolutely, although the truth was that I had little idea of what I was doing.

Looking back on those days, I was shedding my former identity and sense of self, a warped idea of who I was, in search of my deeper essence and a full life. What I knew, because as I was growing up my dad had said it often enough, was that he just wanted me to be happy.

I did too, but what if almost no one is *actually* happy? Hundreds of years from now, anthropologists will puzzle: twenty-first century humans lived in some of the wealthiest societies in history, yet only a minority of us, around a third, report being happy. Why? Of course, we don't need to view the phenomenon from the future. Based on a wealth of research including the Harvard Study of Adult Development, the longest longitudinal study of what actually keeps people healthy and happy, we now have a clearer understanding of the importance of one aspect of fulfilled lives: close relationships. Unfortunately, we in the twenty-first century over-complicate our lives in ways that make close relationships more difficult. Why?

Given such widespread lack of happiness and fulfillment, it is hardly controversial to argue that the dominant paradigms we are living in are flawed, especially in how we view "success." Instead of prioritizing meaningful relationships, many of us live in a highly competitive and transactional world, jousting for resources and status, while spending most of our lives living in largely unacknowledged fear. We fear we'll be seen as inadequate, as vulnerable, as ones who don't belong. And we try to protect ourselves by putting on manufactured personas. I did too, until I discovered one of the portals to the other side of the matrix.

Pretty much everyone who visits Pixar's headquarters in Emeryville, California (just across the Bay from San Francisco) melts into a child-like version of themselves the moment they walk through the front door. Next to the entrance stand two life-sized characters from *Monsters, Inc.*: the towering, lovable, blue-furred monster with horns, a tail, and purple spots—James P. "Sulley" Sullivan—and his goofy and diminutive, bright green, spherical, one-eyed best friend, Mike Wazowski. Adult-sized versions of Woody and Buzz Lightyear from *Toy Story*, built from Legos, stand next to the reception desk. Pixar feels a bit like Disneyland. All around, aside from the giant case of Academy Awards, you are surrounded by art and life-sized characters from Pixar movies—from *Toy Story* to *The Incredibles*.

It's hard to describe the kinship that I felt with Sulley, the legendary "scarer" voiced by John Goodman in *Monsters, Inc.* I'm not saying I aspired to be a professional scarer. I'm just saying I could relate to Sulley, who was in truth a playful, gentle giant at heart, with an inner child of about six or seven years old. We all need spirit animals, so why not pick a cartoon character that ignited my own inner child? Like him, I could be a bit lazy at times. Yet, also like Sulley, I was a consummate professional once focused.

Walking into Pixar for the Improvibles performance that night, I felt I'd finally found an oasis after my years of crawling through the desert, a place where I could be fully human. A place where I could reconnect with my inner child. I wanted back my imagination and playfulness, which I'd all but lost during those years in a suit while craving some bullshit notion of success. Sulley was comfortable in his own fur. And he prized his relationships, especially that with his partner and best friend, Mike. Sully was my perfect spirit guide.

Walking from the entrance into the cavernous, light, and airy central atrium of Pixar's main building—designed by Steve Jobs—I felt so welcomed. So warm. So alive again. Along with the natural light that flooded the space, human connection and joy seemed to cascade through the building. That was just what Ed Catmull, Pixar's co-founder and the person whose driving passion and vision really started it all, had aspired to nurture. I'd read and watched everything I could get my hands on about Pixar. Now here I was, feeling the positive energy of Pixar's magic. That's when my agonized wandering finally found an oasis after years of crawling through the desert: a place where I could be human.

I had begun to feel the magic even before stepping into the building.

I had just walked through the Pixar security gate and was laughing with a fellow attendee, Martin Giles, the San Francisco Bureau Chief of *The Economist* magazine, about the guest passes, which had an alien on them and read: A Stranger from the Outside. It was so on-brand for Pixar. At that very moment, about forty yards away, an older man walked towards the employee parking lot.

"Hold up," I said, staring at the shaded figure, challenging disbelief. "*Is that Ed fucking Catmull?*"

By then in his mid-60s, Catmull had an unmistakable gait about him: seemingly deep in thought, yet open to life around him. I had met him once before, very briefly after he had given a lecture at Stanford's computer science school during those lost years.

"Holy shit!" Martin replied, also aghast. "I think it is. Should we?"

Martin had interviewed Ed at some event at UC Berkeley's business school a couple months prior, so he knew him well enough to say hello. After looking at each other briefly, we yelled, "Ed!" while waving our arms.

With that, Ed turned towards us, and waited patiently for us as we walked quickly over, somewhat breathless with excitement. I felt like we were tracking down Bigfoot in his natural environment: the Pixar parking lot.

"Hello, Ed!" Giles said enthusiastically. "We did that session at Berkeley last month."

"Yes! Hello, Martin," Ed replied genially, as if he was Martin's kind uncle, sounding professorial behind his wire-framed specs and salt-and-pepper beard.

All I could think was: Holy shit. Ed Catmull. Bigfoot.

Back when Ed was a Ph.D. student at the University of Utah in the 1970s, he pioneered some early computer-graphics technology, including by drawing his own hand. Ed made it his life mission to create the first full-length, digitally-animated film. People thought he was crazy because the technology to make a digitally-animated film was seen to be decades off. But he assembled a small band of believers and, step by step, making short films, they developed the technology and digital storytelling muscles to make their first full-length feature, *Toy Story*. The quest took ten years longer than Catmull had anticipated, but *Toy Story* was such an enormous hit that it launched a new industry.

I can't remember what I said to Ed after Martin Giles introduced me. I probably mumbled something incoherent. I just remember that Ed spoke in a very matter-of-fact way, with zero pretense, almost as if we knew each other already.

Through the subsequent years, I would learn that that was Ed through and through.

By the time of our conversation in the parking lot, Pixar had made about a dozen films, and nearly all of them were blockbuster hits at the box office. Ed was president of not only Pixar, but also Walt Disney Animation Studios, which had purchased Pixar in 2006, with the hope that Ed and the Pixar team could revive Disney's own magic. None of the success and acclaim had changed Ed's manner or diverted him from his focus on creating exceptional conditions for others to flourish.

The group I'd come to see, the Improvibles, was championed by one of its members, Craig Good, who started at Pixar doing janitorial and security work way back in the early days of the company. He'd made his way up into a variety of roles, defying constraining conventions and bucking expectations, just as Ed hoped Pixar would help all at the company do.

The group's name was a play on the title of Pixar's movie *The Incredibles*, the making of which epitomized the Pixar magic. Its director, Brad Bird, was so ambitious in his concept for the film that the technical team said making it would be far too expensive. Animating the drawings of water, fire, and hair would be hard enough, let alone the massive number of sets that would be required. It might cost $500 million, some said. Bird scoffed at the skepticism, and instead put a call out:

> "Give us the black sheep," Bird exhorted. "I want artists who are frustrated. I want the ones who have another way of doing things that nobody's listening to."

Having always felt like a bit of a lonely misfit, the idea that being a black sheep was no mark of shame, but instead the result of rebellious creativity, resonated deeply with me. I didn't think of myself as a black sheep, but I hoped I could become one.

Throughout those wandering years, one of the things I lacked was a good support structure that was less transactional—those who could understand the creative path and support me on it. The agonizing feeling of being alone and so lost fueled a passion to find a group of fellow travelers. That night at Pixar, that group began to spontaneously coalesce.

The Improvibles performance was so energizing, so playful and collaborative and, well, improvisational, that as a group of about six of us stumbled joyously out of Pixar's front gate after-wards, we decided to keep the fun going. Turning down Park Avenue, we spotted the blue neon sign of Rudy's Can't Fail Cafe.

"It's a sign!" someone shouted, and we all laughed as he took a photo of the sign with his phone for posterity.

The Can't Fail Cafe was a classic diner yet featuring art on the walls and blasting punk music—the perfect hangout for a Pixar-inspired initiation into embracing our inner black sheep. We learned later that the place was part-owned by Green Day's bass player, Mike Dirnt, and was named after The Clash song *Rudie Can't Fail*. The staff put three or four tables together for us, and we bonded over comfort food and laughter. That's what I remember most: a bunch of adults just laughing. We were freed from the constraints and worries of modern life by this magical place called Pixar that encouraged each of us to let our inner children come out and play.

We talked quite a bit about the whole "black sheep" thing; how that was the way to be, and how we'd all really like to be.

And suddenly it hit me: we could establish a Black Sheep movement. We could speak to the artists within people, helping them bring out their imaginative, playful inner children that needed to be uncorked, somehow helping create the support structure of fellow travelers that I so craved. I would love to do that; it would be an exciting, fulfilling, and *fun* mission. It was powerfully aspirational and human. Sitting there, my mind started to connect dots around how we could get the ball rolling. I was sure lots of people would want to be involved.

"You know," I raised my voice to be heard over the cacophony of separate conversations, "I think this Black Sheep thing could be huge!"

CHAPTER TWO

THE
DARK WOOD

A decade before that night, I was literally (and metaphorically) on the other side of the world from Pixar, inside the matrix. Back then, in the early aughts, I was working in the bowels of what you might call the "white-sheep world," chasing sugar water inside the capital markets of London. That was when I first found myself in a dark wood.

"Tired and uninspired," the voice said, a metronome inside my head. Vanished was the spring in my step of that suit-wearing, boss-pleasing, eager beaver. I could barely drag myself out of bed when the BBC clicked on at 7:00 in the morning. Something felt very wrong; somewhere an unlit part of my soul screamed, "Oh, crap!"

"What the hell?" I demanded, at a loss to comprehend. *"You should be happy!"*

"You're a very successful person!" my mind exclaimed.

After all, I was devoted to that wonderfully abstract claim: success. And I was a better example of having made it than many of those keen to achieve. London was on the other side of the world from where I grew up in Northern California.

But I just wanted to be *human*.

Before my crisis of meaning hit me, I was one diligent bastard. I was determined to "make it" inside the opaque world of venture capital and live up to my Brooks Brothers' suits' good name. There I was, just twenty-six, living in a swanky flat in London's upscale Holland Park, thanks to the pretty penny my firm, Summit Partners, paid. Always the first one to the office and usually the last to leave, I was so much more than a dedicated little soldier. I was vanguard; I was cutting edge; I was the future. The firm had sent a Partner and me to London to start their European office. I was a "suit."

A "suit" is exactly what I, at age twenty-six, wanted to be, yet not. I wore the suit proudly, but in retrospect I was more of a mole, a sleeper cell deep inside the matrix we call the "capital markets," gathering intel and allies while preparing for a future role with a rebel alliance.

We were all what you would call "insecure overachievers." I wouldn't hear that term for another ten years, when a former partner of Bain Consulting mentioned it to me. I subsequently learned that McKinsey & Co. was in the habit of seeking out a similar profile in its recruiting. My colleagues and I fit the definition. We put the "over'" in "overachiever," and no one is driven to achieve that much deal-making without a healthy dose of insecurity. I mean, it's not like we were saving lives. Venture capitalists are driven primarily by two things: extreme competitiveness and money. But behind both was something else.

Turns out, a professor at Cass Business School in London, Laura Empson, spent years studying the psychology of insecure overachievers. She summed us up: "Insecure overachievers are exceptionally capable and fiercely ambitious, yet driven by a profound sense of their own inadequacy."

Back then, I treasured accolades and distinctions, like being considered the Top Associate or getting selected to start the London office. Sure, experiencing London was a life-changing experience for a kid from a small town. But the experience wasn't the point. The achievements weren't the point. Being identified with them was. If I started feeling down, I might actually pull up my résumé. At a low point I confessed this to my brother, who did a double-take. And let's face it: it was beyond bizarre. I was always seeking the next award, achievement, or morsel of praise and validation from my bosses—something to help me feel significant, secure, whole. Something to keep me from confronting the fact that I had almost no idea who I really was beneath the hood.

"You wer-k too much!" Marie, my French girlfriend, would say in her adorable accent. Obviously, she was right. I was spent.

Marie did not wer-k too much. She had a chill beach soul from Saint-Tropez and an energetic, warm smile. She radiated a free-spirited vibe that slightly resembled that of Bridget Bardot. All of those characteristics combined to make her a wonderful antidote to the work week. When we'd lie in the park on those rare, warm London days, with my head nestled in her lap, I'd gaze up into her tranquil, brown eyes and they would soothe me like the waters of the Mediterranean Sea.

On Friday and Saturday nights we'd almost always danced. Unlike me, often dressed like a bad Gap advertisement, Marie looked chic without fail. I had never dated someone so fashionable, who worshiped Madonna no less. But there we were, London lovebirds. Her English was good, while my French got only marginally better. The only time we had trouble communicating was when we talked by phone. Even our struggles to be understood were kind of funny, a virtue of our being in the throes of romance.

Our song was *[I've Had] The Time of My Life*, which was recorded by Bill Medley and Jennifer Warnes. We'd dance for an hour or two, until our clothes were drenched with sweat, which was as good a cue as any to go home and make love. It was all very sweet and completely ridiculous at the same time.

"You're living the dream!" my head would pronounce, although the rest of me increasingly complained that I obviously wasn't. On the surface, I was very successful at embodying the idea of success. My body didn't care.

At about the two-year mark of 75-to-85-hour work weeks in London, shit really started to hit the fan. My body was running on fumes; my soul felt crushed. "Tired and uninspired," just kept repeating inside my head.

I woke up naturally around 6:30 a.m., but usually felt I could sleep another 2-3 hours. Instead, I'd look at my watch every five or so minutes, waiting for my 7:00 wakeup call: the BBC radio news. I'd hit the snooze button and lie in bed motionless for another ten minutes. While no one topic consistently ran through my mind, most of what I thought about was how tired and fatigued my body felt. Sometimes I would think, "Maybe I should just call in sick." Other times, something more primal: *"Screw this!"*

The three-story, 1720s townhouse where I worked, 8 Clifford Street in Mayfair, had a gorgeous facade and complicated inner life. Inside, it was one of the classiest buildings I had ever seen. A wood-framed staircase wound up and to the right of a sprawling mural, a "monochrome trompe l'oeil," whatever the hell that meant. It stretched up to the ceiling, some twenty feet high, and was attributed to Sir James Thornhill, the famous 18th century English painter. At the first landing, on the left, was the nicest of the eight conference rooms in the building. Each room was colored differently and decorated with antiques—from tables to the chairs to bookcases to the paintings on the walls. Everyone seemed to love the building. It commanded respect.

As you made your way towards the back of the building, however, you would notice something odd. Connected to the back of this beautiful, historic building was a modern office wing. Half of the building's offices, and all of the conference rooms, were in the classy townhouse, while the back half looked Euro-modern. It all worked once you got over the shock, and a schizophrenic workplace seemed, in a word, apt. Our little piece of it was on the 4th floor of the modern Euro appendage, about one thousand square feet in total, not including the roof deck.

I would arrive first, at 8 a.m. My days would usually finish just after 10 p.m. On the Tube ride home, I would often come close to falling asleep. On Tuesday nights, the fuel of the weekend utterly spent and the stretch of the work week ahead, I would stare at my reflection captured starkly in the darkened window opposite my seat and ask myself, "Why am I doing this?" My inner monologue would continue: "I am deeply fatigued. I have almost no energy." In those moments, I tried to change the subject. "You are so damn tired; you can't think objectively." Oftentimes, this dissolved into an argument with myself, after which I would conclude, "This is not sustainable."

Pretty much everyone, including my parents, Aunt Liz, Uncle Joe, and my college friends, thought I had a cool job. My mother was mainly happy that I could experience London as a young man, while Dad regaled in telling friends that his eldest son worked at a global venture capital firm. This was, after all, the early 2000s: the dot-com boom meant a presumption of endless heydays for venture capital. Seemingly everyone wanted in, wanted a job in the industry. Our firm, Summit Partners, was hot too, selected in that turn-of-century year as one of Red Herring's Top 25 Venture Capital Firms of 2000. That was the year one of the firm's investments in a technology company made Summit Partners a profit of $4.2 billion. That's right: the firm made a $4.2 billion profit on *one* investment!

My boss, Scott Collins, was ten years my senior, had just made Partner, and took the whole overachiever thing to insane levels. Collins grew up in Chicago, then went to Harvard College, where he played linebacker for the football team, before continuing on to Harvard Law School. After that came stints at the White House and McKinsey & Co. And then he landed in venture capital.

He always seemed like he was about to blow a gasket. His pale blue eyes darted laser-like around any room, his glare framed by his protruding, square jaw, his brain a warehouse of wry one-liners. We made for a conspicuous yet effective odd couple. My soul was California, an echo of Marie's chill beach soul; Scott's soul was Chicago, gritty, intense. Like the Chicago Bears' legendary Hall of Fame middle linebacker Mike Singletary, Scott rarely blinked.

Simply: Scott was the most intense, hardest-working person I had ever known. His great sense of humor was a godsend, but he just took things to a whole other level. I knew that someday he'd run the whole firm, but right then Scott Collins was running Peter Sims. And Peter Sims lived for praise, accolades, and achievements.

One Tuesday night, for instance, I was still getting emails from him at 11:30 p.m. It wasn't unusual for him to email late at night like that, after his (four!) kids were asleep. But we had a 7 a.m. flight scheduled for the next day, and both of us had to wake up around 4:45 a.m. I was trying to finish everything before three days of travel, and Collins was sending me emails about leads we were working on—not high priority stuff. True, the more leads we processed, the more likely we would make our first European investment, but Tuesday night and, at best, the hope of four and a half hours of sleep?

My reaction in situations like these was always, "Man, this guy must *really want it*." But did *I* want it?

Scott was in a particularly stressful position. He was under enormous pressure to secure our first European deal, especially because the new office wasn't cheap. Yet moments like that Tuesday night caused me to question everything about my career path and, well, my life.

Beneath the pressure, the darting, unblinking eyes, and the midnight intensity, Collins had a good heart and great sense of humor. In airports and pubs, he softened over a couple beers, and I got a good sense for his inner monologue. I remember one day when the office manager for the law firm that occupied most of our building announced she was leaving London on what seemed to us a whim. She and her husband were moving to the Cayman Islands. It was a complete shock. We adored Alison; she was effervescent and endlessly charming, full of down-to-earth warmth and an easy hospitality. She was like family, these two American suits' one true English friend. But there it was: boom!

She and her husband had had it with the London weather and cost of living. Her husband landed a job with a Cayman law firm and off they went.

After work that day, Scott and I went to a local restaurant, and after a few beers Scott blinked. "Maybe Alison's figured out something that we haven't . . ." he said as his voice trailed off with the comment. From our seats, we stared out onto a rain-soaked cobblestone alley.

We lived with that feeling all the time. The gnawing sense that somewhere out there, beyond London's weather and cost of living, there was another world, another way of living that was, perhaps, better than ours. This thought, I came to appreciate, routinely goes through the heads of people working in the bowels of finance. Maybe, just possibly, the ski bum in Park City, the yogi in Bali, or that poet at the bar has figured out a better way to live. And sometimes they obviously have!

Words like "happiness" and "fulfillment" don't float around the hallways of the ultra-competitive world of high finance. We were classically insecure overachievers, all of us. You feel good when your "deal," your investment, closes, yet for only a week, maybe two. Then you need to find your next deal to feel a sense of purpose again, as a steady sonic of fears of failure and inadequacy repeats softly from a deep-subconscious DJ booth. Oh—and you're only as good as your last deal. Many investors, and unfortunately nearly all were men, sustained a focus on their families, strove to balance purpose in their lives, and in my firm most remained dedicated to their wives and kids. I worked with some great people with good hearts. But we were all insecure overachievers, "deal guys" who moved from one transaction to the next, masters of selling, hiding information, and manipulation.

"Would you run over your grandma for this one, Simsie?" a colleague once asked me, as he erupted with laughter.

That was an inside joke: in such a competitive industry, you basically need to be willing to sacrifice almost everything to close a hot new deal.

Humor was our elixir and creative outlet. We joked, finagled a lot of pranks, fostered a camaraderie that made the days and weeks manageable, even enjoyable. And we affectionately called each other by the last name, with an "ie" attached: Simsie, Burnsie, DeCoonsie, Mossie. But the analogy that we were hamsters chasing the next drop of sugar water was completely appropriate. And there was never enough sugar water. In a highly competitive world like venture capital, you mostly end up as an idea of who you are, protected by your ego.

Externally, of course, the presentation was always "We're successful. We have it all figured out." It *had* to be. Our identity, our image, depended on it, and our greatest fear was failing that image of success. But we mostly lived in an echo chamber and didn't get out and into the rest of the world much. Surrounded by each other, the industry, which boiled down all of us toiling within it for 70 to 85 hours a week, acted as its own self-contained force field. It's powerful. We talked a lot about our achievements, wore big watches, and hid behind our titles and the prestige of our firm.

But we were all running from something. I was running from feeling so alone as a kid, someone who didn't fit in with any group, and towards what I thought would earn me love and admiration—perhaps from my dad, perhaps from my peers. Inside, soft voices whispered that there must be another way to live rather than be one of the countless sheep in their suits on the Tube platform. Perhaps Alison and her husband *had* figured out something that we hadn't.

I'll never forget the night I was working late in the Boston office during my first year with the firm. Our offices were downtown, high up in the Federal Reserve Building overlooking South Central Station. It was about 5 or 6 p.m., a time I used to think of as the beginning of "the second shift." The firm had about 100 applicants for every Associate job opening. Not only had I landed the job; I wanted to be the best Associate out of about twenty-five in the firm. I sustained my spiritual curiosity, even though I had little time for reflection. So I sought out little moments.

Standing in a Partner's office that night, I looked down on all the people far below, streaming like ants around South Station. I wondered what their lives were like, and how they found meaning. The Partner joined me at his window and I shared my curiosity. Who were all these people? What were their lives like?

"Suckers!" he quipped, with a playful chuckle.

That about sums up the firm's—the industry's—self-contained force field: if you were "in," you were considered part of a special club, a beneficiary of a prestigious identity. If you were "out," you were a sucker, or worse: an idiot, especially if you chose to leave the firm to do something completely different. After all, back then everyone wanted to work in venture capital. There were billion-dollar deals to close, windfalls of cash to reap. One of the Associates in the Boston office was a Harvard-trained doctor who left medicine to work in venture capital. On any medical or pharmaceutical question he was brilliant, yet he struggled to understand how to assess potential investments, let alone close them. He had been trained to save lives, but that ability was now a liability. One of my colleagues called him "the dumbest smart guy in the world."

That word "success" is a marvelous abstraction, isn't it? That is, until you ask yourself over and over (and over) what that word actually means to you.

❧

Fortunately, there was another Scott at 8 Clifford Street: Scott Burns. He provided perspective each day in London: a glimpse of the other side of the matrix. Scott Burns was the founder and Managing Partner of the London office of Brown Rudnick, a Boston law firm and the building's main tenant. We sublet our little office from them. On the surface, Burns sported a somewhat typical corporate lawyer biography. He was a graduate of Brown University and Boston University Law School, and had served as the general counsel to a couple finance companies before becoming the CEO of a $700 million commercial real estate property company for seven years. He had since been a senior partner at his law firm. *And* he was on the boards of directors at Brown University, the Rhode Island School of Design, the Rhode Island Zoological Society, and the Massachusetts Horticultural Society.

If you were to ask Scott Burns who he really was behind his résumé, he would tell you: "I'm weird" or "I've got a lot of quirks" or "I'm crazy" or, my favorite, "I'm a nut!" I had never met a corporate lawyer, let alone so obviously successful a corporate lawyer, who described themself in such ways. And Burns was a man of eclectic interests. He loved antiques, and on busy days he asked that all calls be held, except for calls from Christie's. He spent over a year collecting art and furniture for 8 Clifford Street, and I guessed he had spent about half a million dollars on this collection, for what he considered good value. For the main conference room, he even managed to buy a dozen gorgeous leather chairs from Sting (*that* Sting) for £10,000. He also loved flowers and often got up early to buy roses, tulips, and exotic flora for the office or for his wife, whom he doted on. One junior lawyer told me that when he and Burns went to Stockholm for work, Burns insisted on doing some sightseeing between 6 a.m. and 8 a.m., before their morning meetings. Meanwhile, one day he invited me to meet him at a dog show in London. I said "maybe," but then asked how I would be able to find him there. Without missing a beat, he said, "Just whistle!" That was Scott Burns.

Dogs just fascinated him. One summer night not long after I arrived in London, he took me and one of his interns (a German guy named Friedaman) out to dinner at a French bistro. As Friedaman was describing his childhood, Burns became distracted—a not infrequent occurrence. "I'm sorry to interrupt, but I don't think I've ever seen a dog like that," he said, pointing across the street at a giant dachshund—certainly the largest dachshund I had ever seen.

After a long, admiring gaze, Burns reflected, "That is really an amazingly big dog." Scott Burns' life was full of moments like that: long pauses, awe-inspired observations, playfulness, friendships, and moments just savored.

On summer weekends, Burns rode around on a push scooter (basically a skateboard with a post and handlebars—the kind kids loved back then). "A well-made German one too!" he exclaimed. Burns even rode the thing to the office some days, saying it was a great source of exercise. Mostly, however, he drove around in a 1963 Morris Minor Traveller, a boxy English station wagon that looked like those surfing cars with wood paneling on the sides. His more refined and classier wife, Cindy, was embarrassed as hell about the car, but Burns paid $10,000 for a couple of them and shipped one back to the United States.

The more I learned, the more obvious it was that Scott Burns was not like the rest of us sheep. Prior to moving to London to start that office for his firm, he commissioned the famous conceptual artist Sol LeWitt to paint the walls behind the Boston offices' reception desk. Apparently it was a black and white mural that cost something like fifty thousand dollars, which Burns saw as a bargain since it was "a BIG wall," as he put it by email. Nonetheless, some partners were outraged, and several refused to even speak with Burns again. As for the mural? It remained. People were afraid to paint over it after the enormous expense. Long before I could put a name to it, I began to understand that among us sheep, Burns was a black sheep.

There was also the day when Alison walked into Burns' office and instead of using one of her usual nicknames for him like Scotty or Scooter, she called him Bruno. She claimed later that Bruno just popped into her head. Alison was charming and warm enough to get away with pretty much anything, but that day was different. As soon as she said "Bruno," Burns looked up from his papers, noticeably startled, and told her to close the door. She did. With shock in his eyes, he asked her to sit down, took a deep breath, and began to tell her a story.

Turns out, when Burns was a boy, growing up in Cambridge, Massachusetts, nearby there was a pet bear named Bruno. Yes; that's right: a pet bear. A pet black bear named Bruno. Bruno was owned by the great grandfather of Scott's future wife, who had apparently rescued the cub in a lumbering region of Maine.

Alison had no words. She learned that Bruno's presence loomed large in Burns' early years—memories he held close to his heart. It was one of those moments and conversations you couldn't script if you tried. But it was a window into the unique life and soul of Scott Burns. Yes; he really grew up around a pet black bear, and yes, he was raised in Cambridge, Massachusetts, which he felt got him started down the "nut" path in life.

And so, as I worked my ass off each week in the heart of the London capital markets with Scott Collins, Scott Burns taught me about living life more fully every time I saw him. Although he was a respected corporate lawyer, his life was full of curiosities, color, and texture that went far beyond titles, money, and his next achievement. He was a black sheep in wolf's clothes. From riding push scooters to going to dog shows to obsessing over ornate antiques and rare flowers, Burns always seemed deeply alive. Like all of us, his life was full of imperfections, shadows, demons, and blemishes that others may have judged, yet he seemed to largely accept. He held them in the same fondness that he did his memories of Bruno the bear.

It would take me years to appreciate that the quality of Burns was unquantifiable. It was also the quality that made Burns understandable to Burns, regardless of whether or not anyone else understood. He was *living*.

Meanwhile, we were basically sheep, motivated more by our fears than living in three dimensions. Just ask Professor Empson. She found insecure overachievers everywhere: lawyers, accountants, consultants, managers, specialists, maybe you, certainly me, working seventy-plus-hour weeks. At the core of this anxious overworking is the fear of being exposed as inadequate or being rejected. These nagging fears often result in the imposter syndrome—the idea that we're going to be discovered as less capable, successful, or amazing than people think.

What I couldn't fully understand back then was that insecure overachievers are wired that way for a reason. The sense of inadequacy often goes back to childhood, ranging from the way we are parented to growing up with a lack of financial, emotional, psychological stability. In my case, my dad prized achievement so much that it felt like the source of his love. He had awards all over his office and our house, from his Eagle Scout award to being class marshal at Harvard Law School, which he explained was like being president of his class. Crucially, he got his addiction to achievement and penchant for accolades from his *parents*.

And breaking the addictions or traumas in our lineage to discover our genuine selves takes real work.

Over beers, the space where we could take off our armor and put down our battle axes, Scott Collins usually wanted to talk more about life than work. Mostly, he got me to talk about my social life, yet once during our first year in London he opened a window, just a bit, on himself. He described how his house had been burglarized in the middle of the night while his whole family was sleeping. His voice cracked and it was obvious he needed emotional support from the spiraling stresses. Beneath the darting blue eyes and tough guy facade, he had a real sensitivity, a gentleness, a humanity about him. You'd rarely see that side of Collins unless you really got to know him, and he you.

He wasn't an outlier, though. Over my nearly four years at the firm, I found that everyone I got to know, especially the toughest tough guys, needed spaces to be human and genuinely connect. It usually required alcohol, but as we opened up it became clear that for so many of us the desire to just connect with our parents (most often sons needing more from fathers) as humans, to free ourselves from the seemingly endless yoke of expectations, would be worth all the accolades and millions.

Now, more than a decade later, I can take a step back. It's remarkable to consider how much of our economic system, our political institutions, and our world is run by insecure overachievers. How can we expect to feel human when the systems and institutions controlling our lives are feedback loops of fear and emotional inadequacy? Let's also recognize and empathize. Every insecure overachiever carries some type of burden or trauma, often buried and carefully hidden from the light of day. They carry painful wounds that often trace back to a deep desire to find safety, acceptance, worthiness, or love. They hunger to be human.

The capital markets system was (and is) an extremely powerful orb. And, as I see it, the biggest reason people stay in the game is that the system has one great, incredibly magnetic quality to it: everything can be measured, down to the last decimal point. Every transaction has a measurable return: you invest $10 million and that investment returns $40 million in three to four years. If you're an investor or a banker, the performance of your transactions or deals goes on your scorecard, just like on the golf course. Tracking this personal scorecard, climbing the leaderboard, was one of the main reasons many of my colleagues, who had created great personal wealth, couldn't retire or step into another line of work.

But what if beneath all that score-keeping, few people seem genuinely happy or fulfilled for a sustained period of time?

The correlations between money and happiness are modest at best. Some of the most cited research in this vein comes from the work of Daniel Kahneman and Angus Deaton at Princeton

University. Utilizing Gallup data from 450,000 US residents, the research showed that emotional well-being doesn't progress beyond an income level of $75,000 a year. With surging inflation, that figure may have increased, but what the research illustrates is simple: money doesn't buy happiness, mostly because people are not good at knowing what will positively influence their emotional well-being.

The whole system runs on sugar water, a matrix perfectly constructed to motivate all of us insecure, overachieving sheep to always run harder, faster, and never feel quite good enough about ourselves. Pause for a second: while I developed endless admiration for entrepreneurs and entrepreneurial capitalism, the most influential economic system operating in our world today—public market capitalism—values money above every other metric. The public markets blindly value money above our well-being or mental health; money above our creativity or inspiration; money above nature; and money before any spiritual faith. Somehow, over the past several hundred years, our ancestors allowed our world to become controlled by a system that doesn't give a shit about us as human beings.

None of this is to say there aren't amazing people inside the system, doing the work they seem born to do. Before leaving for London, my boss in Boston, Marty Mannion, had all the right talents and personal attributes to be a very good investor, and he clearly enjoyed the job. He loved the craft of investing and deal-making and also contributed a large amount of his wealth to philanthropic causes. It's important to qualify that there are many great people like this in the heart of the system, but the capital markets system still doesn't give a shit about us as human beings.

Even with Burns close by and London's endlessly fascinating mosaic, the system finally broke me. By the time my body shut down, I had been sprinting for nearly four years at the firm. Our first European investment earned a profit of about $100 million, establishing the London office for good. The Partners tried to persuade me to stay, but I couldn't. My body and mind were aligned. I wanted to feel fully alive.

I wanted to be *human*, warts and all. And I didn't have a clue as to how to go about it.

Let's face it: we live in a white-sheep world. Now, let me first say that I use the term "white sheep" purely as a literary device. I love sheep in general and have nothing against actual white sheep. Nay; I grew up singing *Mary Had a Little Lamb*, and saying, "Vive le mouton!" It's a metaphor, is all, since it would be unfair to suggest that actual white sheep just follow "the herd," a claim for which I have no evidence. That said, I have witnessed a number of actual black sheep inside herds of actual white sheep, just as a point of empirical fact. Thus, in the spirit of being metaphorically provocative, there are a lot of "enablers" all around us, encouraging us to take "tried and true" paths to white-sheep success including: our parents, girlfriends' parents, friends, and peer groups, not to mention popular culture that celebrates actors and celebrities as gods. Let them go eat hay!

CHAPTER THREE

THE
GATES OF
HELL

There are no excuses. There can be lessons, if there are enough meaningful consequences. But there are no excuses.

That's why Jeffrey Epstein, a devil incarnate, was a figurative Rorschach test for morality within the power structure, the system, at work in the world today, as well as the people inside the institutions that capitulate their so-called noble missions and values for the sake of money. The men—and it is almost always men whose behavior has contributed to hurting so many people— better hope (and pray) that the consequences for bad behavior are as lenient in the afterlife as they are today. One of those men is Leon Black, who, it was discovered, paid Jeffrey Epstein $158 million over the years, ostensibly to help Black reduce his taxes.

While I was working in the trenches in London, the name of another investment firm, Apollo, came up from time to time. The company kept a pretty low public profile, though, and Summit didn't compete with them on deals all that much, so the Partners didn't obsess about Apollo like they did our nemesis: TA Associates. Internally, TA was known as "the bad guys" and the competitor we had to stay most focused on. Apollo Global Management, meanwhile, grew into a $500 billion Wall Street asset-management behemoth. The firm had been co-founded by Leon Black.

Incredibly, Leon Black made those payments to Jeffrey Epstein not before Epstein pleaded guilty to being a sex offender in 2007, but after he had done so. Black nevertheless bankrolled Epstein, which included Epstein's despicable acts that harmed numerous vulnerable young women and children. In the portion of *The Divine Comedy* that describes Hell, Dante Alighieri famously put the most sinful at lower and yet more horrible layers of hellish torment. Epstein deserves to be there. Arguably, his enablers should be a level or two beneath him. One of the things l'affaire Epstein revealed was how many of America's leading cultural and educational institutions are in bed with wealth. If you're wealthy enough, you still get invited to the fancy New York City galas and events. And while wealth and evil do not go hand-in-hand, evil can hijack wealth and leave a taint on the institutions' wealth supports.

Tellingly, Black wasn't asked to step down as Chairman of the Museum of Modern Art when it was first believed he had given "only" $50 million—the first public estimate—to Jeffrey Epstein. Then there was the internal Apollo investigation. Only after that investigation revealed that Black had given Epstein

$158 million for tax avoidance advice was Black finally made to step down as chairman. Yet the leadership of the Museum of Modern Art, one of America's leading cultural institutions and supposedly an exemplar of civilization, still allows Black to sit on its board. Behavior like this is acceptable only in the white-sheep world, where money routinely trumps morality.

When society, the system, reveres money as the be-all and end-all of success, and when "greed is good" gets conflated with masculine strength, power, and prowess, it comes as little surprise that some of the most ruthless people at the heart of our capital markets system live with deep fears and feelings of inadequacy. To take that lesson isn't to excuse evil, but a step towards preventing its spread. Because until we start rejecting the idea that making (or having) money as our main (maybe even sole) definition of success, we are all enablers in some way.

Most humans have no trouble declaring that fraud is wrong, stealing is immoral, and abuse is cruel. The fact is, however, that there aren't many consequences for some of the worst-behaved, wealthy, and powerful people. That is true around the globe, although America has been especially lenient, recalling that oft-heard reminder that not one senior banking executive went to jail in the wake of the near-implosion of Wall Street that led to the Great Recession.

You can even find some of these assholes roaming in the wild, gallivanting around New York City streets and London fundraisers. One Saturday morning in 2013, for instance, at an event for entrepreneurs held on the floor of the New York Stock Exchange, I ran into none other than Dick Fuld, the former CEO of Lehman Brothers, as he knuckle-walked past me. I use the term "knuckle-walked" affectionately since Fuld was known as

"The Gorilla" of Wall Street, notorious for his legendary competitiveness and intensity. Seeing the silverback up close on the floor of the Exchange was a surreal moment.

It was about five years after the Lehman bankruptcy, so at first I couldn't believe it was actually him. Shouldn't he be under a rock somewhere? Shouldn't he be in jail? But there was no mistaking his scowl. He walked with a measured gait, as he carefully scanned the scene, like a fallen boxer re-entering the ring. Overtaken by curiosity, I extended my hand while saying, "Dick," and introduced myself. His hard scowl immediately melted into a smile, and he relaxed, seemingly delighted to encounter a friendly face. We spoke for about ten minutes.

As evidence that the universe has a sense of humor, or at least the universe I was tuned into, while Fuld talked it occurred to me that he looked quite a bit like Grand Moff Tarkin, the Imperial Commander of the Death Star in *Star Wars* (played by Peter Cushing). And what I took to be the thought of my childish imp, I couldn't help the irony: wait—didn't Tarkin go down with the Death Star after Luke Skywalker and the Rebel Alliance blew it up? (But I digress, pulled by what I can understand only as my own adorable pomposity.)

After Lehman blew up, Fuld did not go down with the ship and go to jail, even though a bankruptcy court examiner described their use of controversial accounting techniques as "actionable balance sheet manipulation" and "accounting gimmicks." According to the examiner, the point of those techniques was to make Lehman Brothers' balance sheet look $50 billion smaller during the first and second quarters of 2008, or right before the bank collapsed. Lehman's atrocious risk management and devious accounting practices could not have been more clear. There's a word for it: fraud. When it all imploded, Fuld was the CEO and Lehman closed its doors 158 years after it was founded, all while nearly bringing the world economy down with it. So the Death Star analogy isn't far off, except that gross incompetence rather than any Rebel Alliance triggered the planet-wide fiscal implosion.

That's why I was surprised Fuld wasn't in jail but instead prowling the Stock Exchange on a Saturday morning. What was more, he was reportedly worth between $150 million and $200 million, with mansions in Sun Valley, Florida, and Greenwich, Connecticut. Meanwhile, his wife, Kathleen, is also still on the Museum of Modern Art board, alongside Leon Black—clearly a safe haven for white sheep.

Our conversation started with some small talk about my work and the new merchant bank that Fuld started, literally called Matrix Private Capital. I guess you could say it was a bit like running into Smith in the heart of the matrix. I'm not going to lie; at that moment, I felt a bit like Neo in the movie *The Matrix*, fighting for all the "little people" like Uncle Joe and Aunt Liz and the people I grew up with who were still processing the enormous pains from the Great Recession. But I wanted to get past the courtesies. I was curious to find out what several years of reflection might have produced in the way of Dick Fuld's "lessons learned." So at a natural point in the conversation, when we hit a lull in the pleasantries, I asked him if we (all of us) had learned anything from the crisis. I was somewhat surprised by his emphatic response: "Nothing! Not at all!"

It took me a beat to fully understand what he was trying to convey: the silverback was upset that no one had learned a damn thing from Lehman going down the drain and nearly taking the global economy with it. Well, maybe not no one. A whole lot of suffering Americans, including my Uncle Joe and Aunt Liz, had learned some extremely painful lessons. The bottom 50% of wealth holders in the United States lost 42% of their net worth during the Great Recession. It's no wonder they learned to distrust "the system." But what had the damn silverback and all the other unrepentant beasts roaming around Wall Street learned?

I asked Fuld if he'd be willing to speak out about what we could all learn from the meltdown and the crisis. He said that he would like to do so eventually. That made sense. There were still open investigations. Yet by September 2013, just a few months after our conversation, an eight-member SEC Lehman Brothers team unanimously agreed to end its investigation, just as the FBI also came up empty on a parallel criminal case, bringing a halt to their efforts, right before the statute of limitations for most charges expired. The SEC team argued that Fuld did not know Lehman was using questionable accounting techniques, despite testimony from another Lehman executive who suggested otherwise.

No one went to jail. The Gorilla roams free.

But that Saturday in New York City, the cloud of some possible legal retribution still hung over Fuld, providing him reasons for not saying anything more publicly. After asking for my card, he did offer a final thought, though. Fuld was convinced that America's debt levels were unsustainable and that the country would ultimately have to default on its debts. I was stunned.

"You mean like Argentina?" I asked, to which he nodded.

That was depressing—and a little terrifying—so I said, perhaps naively, "That can't happen. This is America."

That's when he got fired up. True to his nom de guerre, Fuld's eyes flamed and his body tensed as he literally put his finger into my chest and said: "I tell you what. When someone owes you money and they can't pay it, you get screwed!" This was a subject Fuld knew intimately. "There is no way we can afford all of this," he fumed on the floor of the Exchange, "and it's only a matter of time. The government is totally screwed up. It's a total mess!"

Although I was taken aback by his sudden aggression, I realized it was a classic power tactic from one of Wall Street's former titans. (I also later learned that gorillas also rely on upper-body striking techniques.) After helping spark a global economic meltdown, the Gorilla seemed to suggest he was a victim. Yet Fuld seemed to feel anything but powerful that day. When I asked him what he could do to help solve America's problems, he said he used to be able to get things done with the snap of his fingers. Not anymore. There was a vulnerability, and with it a crack open for some compassion. I appreciated that moment. Maybe there was hope, I thought. There should always be space for redemption, for everyone, even Fuld. Although Fuld seemed like he needed a tranquilizer and perhaps some prison time first.

I'm sure he carries heavy demons, constantly worrying about how he stacks up against a group of people he competes with for status. If your life is built upon transactions, it can quickly become its own private Idaho: layer after protective layer of persona with few real friends. When Fuld finally did emerge for a public speech in 2015, after years of silence, he gave a rambling speech at a conference in Manhattan, ending on an eyebrow-raising note. "What did Sigmund Freud say? 'You can say whatever you want about me. I'm okay because I know my mother loves me,'" he said to a crowd of 1,300 financial professionals. "And my mother still loves me. She's 96."

I'm sure Freud would have a field day with Fuld, and all of the "masters of the universe" who run much of the capital markets at the heart of capitalism. When winning supersedes humanity for a lifetime, this is what you get: enough is never enough; every slight or provocation becomes fuel to fight, compete, and flex. But at least your mother will still love you.

CHAPTER FOUR

A CREATIVE RENAISSANCE

By the night the group of us bonded over connecting to our inner black sheep at Pixar and the Can't Fail Café, I had experienced how powerfully so many people all around the country and world were seeking to break free from the matrix. I had finally gotten my footing again, having started a new life as a writer. On the tour for my book *Little Bets*, about unleashing creativity, I met countless people who felt crushed by the system, whether it was inside their company or creative types trying to make a living. Even so, I was surprised by the response to the whole Black Sheep idea.

After that night, I had Black Sheep hats and t-shirts made up and began sharing them with friends. When a group of us went for drinks in our hats at the Black Sheep bar on Polk Street in San Francisco, people kept coming up to us saying they'd love a hat. Wherever I went wearing one of them, people from all walks of life asked me where they could get one—from my Uncle Joe to Beth Comstock, who was then the Chief Marketing Officer at GE, to Wyclef Jean of Fugees fame, whom I ran into at a charity event in New York. They all said they felt like black sheep, and had for years. "Where have you been all my life?" people would often ask me. Then they'd share that they had been feeling isolated, alone, and, well, lonely. It was as if a global tribe of misfits existed who had always been eager to belong.

An underlying yearning, it seemed, to use Beth Comstock as one example, was the desire to have more fun and be a bit more creative and human, if for only a short window. Let me explain: Beth was surely an over-achiever, having made it to the top of one of the biggest companies in the world, yet she also constantly searched for her deeper humanity (and artistry). It seems next to impossible to do both simultaneously. Black sheep inside big companies need to sacrifice a big part of themselves, unless they are the founder or in a purely creative role.

I got a window into Beth's daily life and context when she invited me to join an innovation advisory board to advise GE's new ventures. On a typical day, she spent a lot of time doing financial and leadership reviews, meeting with vendors, and managing politics. Sitting in GE's boardroom high up inside 30 Rockefeller Plaza felt a bit like being in the cockpit, except without the personality and vibe. GE's culture was like that: not much soul or feeling; instead, it was very heavily bent on engineering and finance. Most conversations and meetings were quite analytical and heady, which I found exhausting. GE was basically a completely vibeless culture, out of balance between masculine and feminine, with a notable exception being Beth and her posse of black-sheep colleagues.

What was particularly unique about Beth was her wide-ranging curiosity across many domains—including technology, art, design, history, and culture—a thirst for discerning patterns in the world that might point the way to the future. As the Chief Marketing Officer, she became the face of not just tired, old, white-guy-centric GE, but also the vanguard of a new generation of corporate innovators who weren't afraid to try a lot of new things. And it seemed like everyone—from the C-suites of corporate America to grassroots innovators in places like Louisville or Detroit—liked and respected Beth.

The way I came to see it, she was almost an accidental business leader (an assessment she agreed with). After starting her career in media and public relations, she ended up at GE when the company acquired NBC, where she worked. She ended up working for those companies for twenty-seven years and eventually became Vice Chair of GE overseeing innovation—one of the company's top, say, five executives out of roughly 175,000 employees. She had come a long way from her hometown of Winchester, Virginia, in the Shenandoah Valley. It was easy to picture her as one of those down-to-earth all-Americans: the good-girl-next-door, the cheerleader, the Girl Scout, and the good student. But she was also the daughter of an artist. Beth had a glamorous facade and a complicated inner life, which may explain why she joyfully embraced her first Black Sheep shirt and enjoyed hanging out with us.

Like other black sheep in the all-too-often soul-crushing corporate world, Beth embraced a tribe of fellow misfits. One reason that kept her inside a big company, aside from that it was the world she knew, was that she wanted to make a positive impact, and GE had an enormous platform. She was especially

41

passionate about the environment and created an effort inside GE called Ecomagination, which pledged $15 billion in cleaner-technology investments and led to the creation of over a billion new smart meters and a dramatic increase in fuel cell installations, while 50% of all new electric power additions were renewables by 2020.

Anyhow, given the enthusiastic response to the hats and t-shirts and our motley crew, I started bringing together artists, musicians, social innovators, business leaders, and startup founders for Black Sheep dinners. I had met some of them while researching *Little Bets*, including Frank Gehry, the architect, and on a warm fall night in Los Angeles in 2012, Gehry expressed a powerful idea that inspired me and a core group of our growing tribe to take first tentative steps toward trying to build some kind of broader movement.

Then in his 80s, Gehry had become the most famous living architect by the time I interviewed him for the book, widely acclaimed for his designs of the Guggenheim Bilbao Museum, as well as Walt Disney Concert Hall in Los Angeles. He had spent most of the time sketching on a yellow notepad as he told me about how his vision for Disney Hall came together. He came across as a chill guy, with a down-to-earth and aw-shucks persona that barely hid a wild creative spirit.

I had invited him to the dinner of about a dozen people, including filmmakers, entrepreneurs, and a comedian at the Primitivo Wine Bistro in Venice Beach because I knew he lived close by in Santa Monica. I had guessed that he came mostly because he got some good press from *Little Bets*, including in *The New York Times*. Yet it soon became clear that Gehry too had long felt like a black sheep.

Gehry's life story was especially fascinating. He had been a fairly conventional architect until his 50s, surely working in the white-sheep world. Up until a midlife awakening, he designed fairly traditional shopping malls in Santa Monica and suburban LA homes without much personality—all certainly forgettable compared to what came next. While he was designing these unexceptional buildings, he was also hanging out with artists, including those around Venice Beach, and he loved learning from them. Then, around 1978, when he was about 48 or 49 years old, Gehry decided to start tinkering with his house at 1002 22nd Street in Santa Monica. It became a laboratory for expressing his inner artist.

Gehry essentially built a house around the original house. He described how one morning he needed more light while he was shaving, so he took out a hammer and banged a hole in the ceiling to create a new window. His neighbors were apparently pissed off by this approach to home improvement. Gehry kept at it. Call it a midlife crisis or whatever, but Gehry's soul seemed to wake up.

Finding inspiration from artists like Robert Rauschenberg, Jasper Johns, Ed Ruscha, and Richard Serra, Gehry experimented with everything from plywood to chain-link fencing to corrugated metal to plexiglass in encasing most of the original Dutch Colonial bungalow. His whole idea was to build a house constructed from all these new materials *around* the original house. It is one of the most surreal homes you will ever see: the original house peeks through the new exterior of corrugated metal, plywood, chain-link fence, and plexiglass.

Architects call this style "deconstructivism," and it looks like it! But all those experiments informed what would become elements of Gehry's unique architectural voice and style, as exhibited in two billowing metallic wonders: Guggenheim in Bilbao and Disney Concert Hall in Los Angeles. After he turned 50!

Inner artist meets inner child turned architect.

Indeed, Frank Gehry was surely a black sheep. Perhaps it was because he hung out with so many artists in the 1970s that his own artistry came out in his later architecture. Regardless, he would always experience pronounced self-doubt, even after he became the most famous architect in the world. During our conversations he explained that he always felt nervous, even fearful, before starting new projects, afraid he wouldn't know what to do—what he came to accept and call his "healthy insecurity."

"You're never there," Gehry shared, sitting in his studio, as he fretted that no one would remember his work in a few generations.

"*Nooooo*," I countered in disbelief, picturing all the Gehry-imprinted buildings that glimmered, provoked, puzzled, and elevated so many city skylines around the world. "Not even Bilbao or Disney Hall?!" Gehry just shrugged, looking glumly down at his desk. Later, I reflected on how remarkable it was that even Frank Gehry seemed to need a bit of perspective and affirmation.

Meanwhile, Ed Catmull never felt he had made it to "the mountaintop" either—something he accepted, rather than fretted; there was always more to be learned and done.

If there's really no mountaintop of success in life, the journey must truly be the reward.

By the time we were planning that first Black Sheep dinner in Los Angeles in 2012, he agreed to come. We met up at Primitivo Wine Bistro, which was then located in Venice on Abbot Kinney Boulevard. Getting the time wrong, Gehry arrived about thirty minutes early with his long-time chief of staff Meaghan Lloyd. Wondering what all this Black Sheep shit was about, he started to doodle on the paper tablecloth, mapping out his own journey to becoming a black sheep. The sketch started with a little picture of Bar Primitivo, above "WHY," written in all caps, as in, "WHY am I here for this dinner?"

"What the hell is this Black Sheep thing, Peter?" he asked pointedly.

"Well, . . ." I started in, doing my best to explain feeling insecure and unsure, as he glared up from his seat. Most of what we had was a vision.

Since I arrived before the others, I became captivated by Gehry's sketch, and asked him to describe it. Somewhat pained and irritated, he nevertheless went through each part of the sketch. The right-hand side of the drawing had a large school building, which he said represented "traditional school." Just to the left of that, there was a white sheep with a parachute, which he explained was him getting away from the status quo—as in, he had to parachute out of traditional school. Gehry had dropped out of Harvard's Graduate School of Design, "underwhelmed." He had felt that his ideas for socially responsible architecture were unwelcomed there, which no doubt had been part of his decision to leave. There was also a small church with a helicopter drawn just on top of it, as if the helicopter was taking people somewhere else. Gehry didn't talk about that side of the drawing very much, although I knew he had been taunted and bullied in Toronto for being Jewish.

The centerpiece of his drawing, just next to the traditional school, was a white sheep winding its way up a mountain, which Gehry explained was him taking a different path in life. At the top of the mountain was a large black sheep standing beneath a tree, on a patch of yellow. It was the only color crayon he'd used other than black. (I'm guessing he had asked for some of the crayons meant for kids eating at the restaurant.) To my mind, the meaning was clear. The black sheep was standing in the light at the summit of the mountain.

Gehry was clear as to his two core points about becoming a black sheep. One theme was that during his black-sheep journey, he had to go around the whole system, including education and organized religion. The other was that in creating new generations of black sheep, it all came back to education. The journey to the promised land. It was a metaphor of Gehry's quest to his authentic self.

The moment felt unexpectedly significant. Gone were Gehry's insecurities and persona. It was as if I was seeing and hearing his inner artist for the first time. As people started to arrive, his mood brightened. A couple of documentary filmmakers, several entrepreneurs, a comedian, a musician or two, and social entrepreneurs all arrived with great energy. It was a diverse and pretty attractive group—attractive because of the type of creative energy they generated and most anyone would want to be around, including Frank Gehry. As the wine started to flow, the group started to flow, and Gehry started to flow.

"America needs an artistic renaissance!" he shared after about an hour, which again felt like it was coming from a deep place, delivered with almost fist-pounding enthusiasm.

The call resonated with everyone. It fit with the cultural moment and was very inspiring. Yes. Yes! That was it! That's exactly what America needed: an artistic renaissance. Gehry's call for a creative renaissance felt like an antidote to the whole business culture of financializing everything and moral decay.

There was no hierarchy that night: Gehry was just Frank—at least at the beginning of the night. After a while, he told us his nickname was Foggy, and scribbled that on the placemat. Why Foggy, we asked? He was an avid, life-long sailor, since childhood, he explained. Foggy was the name of his sailboat, a place where he could get away and connect with nature and his inner child. Sacred. Sailing inspired his art, I knew, because when he drew out those sketches for me of Disney Hall, he described how his vision for the design resembled a ship with all of its sails open and filled with wind—wing on wing—with both the mainsail and the foresail opened fully.

That evening, we Black Sheep were seeing the real Frank Gehry. The kid who felt free when sailing, who had found his voice in life, and made it big as one of the world's most renowned architects, among the best of his generation. Set the celebrity aside, however, and he was just Foggy—and we all loved him.

As the dinner came to a close, we asked Foggy to sign the placemat, which he did before heading off into the warm evening. People went off in various directions, except for a small group of us who headed towards Venice Beach, ambling, laughing, hugging, and playfully tugging each other towards the ocean where we played on the sand and recounted stories about the night.

Living in an era of endless and soulless individualism, loneliness, celebrity, and consumption, we yearned for genuine connection. We wanted to cut through all the bullshit: all the people and companies who preyed upon our vulnerabilities and insecurities so cynically for their own gains and wealth creation. From the fashionistas using exclusivity to sell belonging to the social-media dons who prey upon our attention, as well as the frailties of our children, we wanted to be part of an insurrection.

America needed a creative renaissance.

CHAPTER FIVE

THE
BELLY OF THE
BEAST

The contrast between the creative tribe that coalesced into the Black Sheep and the brigades working on financializing the world inside the capital markets system was stark. In London, I found myself surrounded by countless investors, bankers, hedge-fund traders, and brokers who weren't creating a goddamn thing yet increasingly held the real political power and access. They lived in places like Greenwich, Palm Beach, London, and Manhattan—places that are packed full of these hedge-fund and LBO dorks. I borrowed the term "LBO dorks"—leveraged buyout dorks—from comedian Hasan Minhaj. He used that term to describe people who use large amounts of debt to buy companies.

I was one of those LBO dorks, fiddling with assumptions in spreadsheets, playing with them to see what "deal" might make the most financial return, even if those keyboard tweaks might include laying off a lot of people. It all falls under the "financialization" of the US economy: a massive shift away from production towards an economy run by financiers. Manufacturing once accounted for 40% of US corporate profits and 29% of its jobs. By the early 2020s, finance accounted for 40% of national profits with 5% of its jobs.

LBO dorks aren't creating a new product or service, and I have never met a hedge-fund manager who can clearly articulate what value they are creating. Investment bankers also focus mostly on selling, except for innovating the sophisticated financial instruments like derivatives that imperiled the entire economy and led to the Great Recession. Not to lack nuance; many people inside the investment world become masters of their craft and live with a strong moral compass.

But the real moral authority in this world doesn't reside inside the financial or political system. It exists in a lot of places you might not expect, within a lot of people who don't even realize how powerful they are (or can be).

Speaking of which: about halfway through my time in London, Aunt Liz, Uncle Joe, and Cousin Nick came for about a ten-day visit. Nick's older sister Jennie, my other cousin, decided not to come on the trip, a significant signal lost in the noise of the fact that this was a big trip, the first time they had ever been to Europe, or ventured that far from our rural Northern California town. My one-bedroom flat in Holland Park was on the other side of the world, the other side of the tracks, and the other side of life. A big "Bob's your uncle!" as the Brits say, or "Et voilà!" as the French say, or "Oh, man!" as Uncle Joe says.

I worked most of the week, but when I finally did see them on the weekend, Uncle Joe was wearing a flannel shirt and Levi's, a look so Uncle Joe he could have patented it. He took pictures everywhere too; loads of pictures; roll after roll of pictures of every building and alley and cathedral that you can imagine, from London to Cambridge.

Cousin Nick was in his adolescence then and identified as something of a punk. I will always remember after about an hour of us walking around Camden Town, with its edgy, sometimes dark-hearted gothic, outlandish market area full of boys and girls sporting mohawks, leather, and chained-up desires. Compared to all that, Nick volunteered, "I am not a punk."

I imagine it was all a bit like The Simpsons touring London.

For as long as I can remember, Uncle Joe began his days with a Thermos full of coffee and ended them with a Coors Light (or Bud Light) wrapped in a koozie. Some friends called him Joe Sixpack—that hypothetical everyman in America—and by my count he had a knack for voting for almost every winning President, until Trump's second try. He was down to earth in a visible, tangible way. By the end of a workday spent moving logs from the forest to the mills, his face, his shirts, and especially his hands and fingernails were caked with dirt. His fingers were giant, not so much long as round. Dad had Uncle Joe's hands cast in plaster, then put them on display in his office. People marveled at them.

In London, Uncle Joe was out of his element for sure, but he wasn't put off his stride. You have a lot of time to think when you're driving a truck. Aside from listening to Bob Seger and The Rolling Stones, Uncle Joe thought a lot about democracy in America. If nineteenth-century philosopher Alexis de

Tocqueville (best known for his legendary tome *Democracy in America*) were alive, he would surely have wanted to ride shotgun for a day with Uncle Joe. The insights, not to mention the entertainment, are priceless.

"Please allow me to introduce myself," Tocqueville might say, for he was a man of wealth and taste.

Uncle Joe would surely respond, "Pleased to meet you. Hope you guess my name!"

Uncle Joe was good like that: a wit as sharp as Mick Jagger's hip. What's more, Uncle Joe's logging truck was a lot more comfortable than the carriages and horses that made Tocqueville saddle-sore as he explored the eastern seaboard states, as well as the then far-west interior of Ohio and Pennsylvania, always witnessing, asking, and scribbling notes. Both Tocqueville and Uncle Joe believed in the potential of a democracy owned by the people. By the end of his trip in 1832, Tocqueville was mostly optimistic. By the early 2000s, Uncle Joe was mostly not.

That didn't dim his sense of humor. Uncle Joe was gifted an old soul and had what I would come to understand as an inner child of about six or seven years old. He was a playful prankster who once built a potato cannon and shot potatoes over a fancy golf course, who could sum up deep insights in a simple phrase or sentence. Uncle Joe was often cracking one-liners he had come up with—usually while driving.

"The internet is just CB radio with pictures," Uncle Joe said, a topic we landed on somehow in a London pub.

It was the type of thought Uncle Joe came up with as he was driving his truck, listening to the other drivers chatter on the short-range CB radio.

"What is CB radio?" a friend asked.

"Ahh, it's just a radio we use to talk with other truckers," Uncle Joe shared with a chuckle. "And a lotta times they have *no idea* what they are talkin' about!"

"What do you talk about?"

"Well, we used to talk about where cops were and stuff like that, but now that people have phones, the CBs don't get used as much," Uncle Joe explained. "But sometimes some jackass starts jabbering about something they know nothing about . . ."

"Wait—do you mean like the stock market?" my friend interjected.

Uncle Joe blurted out a belly laugh. "No, no, no! They *really* don't know *nothin'* about the stock market!"

We were all laughing by then.

"No; they start blabbering about politics or government without knowing *a goddamn thing*," Uncle Joe blurted, clearly enjoying his captive audience. "Maybe repeating something they read on the internet!"

Uncle Joe loved to laugh, and he loved to keep laughing until his whole body seemed to laugh. In that London pub he laughed so hard that his body twisted up in his chair and his hands went up to hold his brow, as if he was about to cry.

"Oh, man!" he said. That was another frequent Uncle Joe-ism.

And that's when those of us who knew him knew he was winding down. He'd withhold his wit and wisdom, usually to let his stomach muscles recover, and to let someone else have the stage.

Not for the first time, and certainly not for the last, I thought if you could bottle Uncle Joe, just maybe you could bridge the distance between where we are now and de Tocqueville's America, a much more "we" version of America, and we'd all be better off.

ⲍ

When you're inside the belly of the beast of the white-sheep world, it can be dark, dank, and hopeless. To switch metaphors, it can be like the long, dark tunnel where the light at the end could be daylight, an oncoming car, or just a brief respite between tunnels. You just hope that you don't snap, but a small part of you worries that one day you just might. A smaller part of you might even welcome the snapping. Let's face it: you don't have any *real* friends at work, or if you do, you're damn lucky. After all, you and your friends usually get together after work to do the things you really enjoy—which is what you're *not* doing while at work. While at work, you can't even really conceive what it would be like to just feel *human*, let alone be at peace with yourself.

You compartmentalize. You suit up your armor, your persona, and take a pull of sugar water. You set another goal: whatever it takes to find another fleeting sense of purpose. You don your armor because it's you versus the world in this lonely universe. Some days, it's like you work in an emotionless Chernobyl without a radiation suit. You just stuff all those basic human needs down into the Siberia of your soul, hoping the No. 4 reactor doesn't explode.

That is, unless you happened to cross paths with Scott Burns in the hallway. Then, blissfully, all bets were off. When I encountered Burns, we were like two over-excited dogs playing at the park, scurrying around with open-mouthed grins and our tongues hanging out. Inside the system with Collins, almost every interaction felt fairly intense and serious, unless it was over beers. Seeing the exception made a difference. Those were years when I imagined life was a lot different for the people at the top of the heap; you know: the people who'd "made it." But those were also the years when I started to wonder if it's only *really* different for the people who somehow say "fuck it" and embrace their full selves, like the self-proclaimed nut Scott Burns.

It took a long time for me to hear my inner child, let alone listen to him, but he had another way of putting it: "being inside the system isn't much fun."

Again, I get it; I really do. When pretty much every interaction is transactional, you spend most of your days talking with people who are likely lying to you in small and large ways. Scott Collins and I used to talk a lot about how full of shit some investment banker or broker was, pitching us their deals, often with smoke and mirrors. Hiding information. Hiding intentions. Hiding who they really were. When survival is primary, there's no space for your inner child to come out and play. You live in constant fear of someone screwing you over or of *losing*—feeling those deep, subconscious, base-of-your-psyche anxieties that motivate the whole system of white sheep and keep inner children locked up in that space beneath the stairs.

When Collins interviewed with Summit Partners, one of the last hurdles he had to clear was to meet with the firm's founding partner, E. Roe Stamps IV. Now, I don't know Stamps' personal story at all, and can only imagine he must have had a lot of emotional burdens and weight, being a "IV" and all. My father, a "III," spent much of his life just trying to be his own man, and it's always hard to know the hidden burdens someone might carry. I met Stamps only once or twice and experienced his Southern charm. Yet his reputation was as one of the toughest sons-of-bitches you'd ever meet in venture capital (or in the world of finance, for that matter). While most of the people I worked with had endless admiration for entrepreneurs, Stamps didn't trust them worth a damn. He worried incessantly about getting screwed over. As best I could tell, Stamps' entire work mindset (and life) centered on winners and losers. One of his heroes was 1960s Green Bay Packers coach Vince Lombardi, who had lots of quotes like: "Winners never quit, and quitters never win."

Lombardi and Stamps would surely say they were all about the team, but Stamps was really all about keeping score, and there were merely winners and losers. It's the type of wounded mindset, rooted in ego and creating separation from others, that too often gets celebrated as strong masculinity.

So E. Roe Stamps IV really had only one question for young Scott Collins: "What describes you best?" he asked. "Do you love winning or do you hate losing?"

Collins nailed it: he hated losing. The fear of failure is a far more powerful motivator than the joy of living.

Back then, neither Collins nor I could imagine a work life that wasn't influenced by competition every day. That whole "us versus them" mindset was a tremendous waste of energy, not to mention lacking in any real spiritual grounding, in contrast to what I would find on the other side of the matrix. That said, given the game we were in, and the blatant culture of deception inside the white-sheep world, Roe Stamps' exhortations to not trust any entrepreneur were often valid.

Once, for instance, an accountant from Ernst & Young in Dublin called me and said that she wanted to introduce Collins and me to one of the finalists for their Entrepreneur of the Year competition in Ireland. "He runs an airline," she said, "a small Irish carrier, but he is completely self-made. He bought the airline for . . ." blah, blah, blah ". . . after he remortgaged his house, and since then the airline has grown from . . ." blah, blah, blah to blah, blah, blah.

"He comes from a very rural town in Northern Ireland, grew up very poor, and still speaks Gaelic with his family," she continued. "He is an inspirational guy and is very down-to-earth." She went on to say he had a good chance to be Ireland's Entrepreneur of the Year. "You ought to meet him," she said. "His company fits well with your investment profile."

A week later, the guy was in London for some air shows and found time to stop by our offices at Clifford Street on the way back to Heathrow. Sitting across an antique wood table from my colleague Sotiris and me, another Scott Burns special, the entrepreneur put his head down and started his pitch. It was almost magical, as if the lights went down and a symphony appeared right behind him. He started from the beginning.

"It was Christmas Day, 1993. And on every Christmas, I go to my wife's parent's house. We eat around 3 p.m. and I then go for a walk around 5:00, by myself, next to the sea. It's a yearly tradition. And that day I walked past an airfield and started thinking, 'There is a lot of potential for air travel in this region.'"

Speaking with his whole body—I mean with, like, every cell and ounce of passion he could find—he talked about how he had mortgaged his house to put up some of the initial funds, along with a partner. Each of the two owned 50%, but the guy in our office, to hear him tell it, did all the work; his business partner merely put up capital. Ever warming to his subject, he went on to describe hiring his first manager. "She was getting paid £9,000 (Irish pounds) a year and I offered to pay her £12,000 if she would take the top job," he described. "After a while, she took it."

At this point, my colleague Sotiris asked how he picked talent. For the next five minutes, the guy got deeply philosophical and made some great points, not all of which were related to Sotiris' question. He said he thought it was important to give people a lot of responsibility, the chance to grow with the company, help them in their personal lives where necessary, and remember that it's all about the team. "People don't work for me; they work *with* me," he crescendoed, and what's more, he said, "What binds it all together is integrity."

Wow! Finally, I thought, here's an entrepreneur who's really humble—and who *gets it*.

As the conversation progressed, however, the cracks widened. We would uncover a few more interesting details. For one, after the first 30 minutes, gone was the head-down humility. There were about thirty to forty "I" statements, such as "I picked all the good air routes" and "I developed the efficient internet ticketing system," for every "we" statement. And then an interesting comment that the company was "really just an instrument to create wealth." Huh. But by far, the most illuminating nuance was that the guy bought out his partner a few years before for about £1 million. That would imply that he had bought 50% of the company at a valuation of £2 million. And after that he had grown the company, and now—in talking to us and our competitors—the company was already worth tens of millions, and he wanted to grow it many times more. If that happened, he would have totally *screwed* his partner.

God bless wealth creation.

Look I get it: when there is a lot of money at stake, most bets are off, but are *all* bets off? I may have been a suit, but I was still trying to hold on to a bit of idealism. I almost laughed out loud when Sotiris said that if this guy did a deal with our firm, he would be able to take care of his personal needs and "keep food on the table." What the hell was Sotiris thinking? The guy's company was already worth a fortune. His plan was to make it exponentially more valuable than that.

Anyhow, at the end of the conversation, Sotiris told the guy it was a great story (which it was) and the guy said, "Well, it's from here," as he tapped on his heart. The whole thing was pretty amusing, a window into our daily life in the London matrix.

Let me be clear. I didn't and don't think the entrepreneur was a bad guy, not at all. But my inner idealist felt that familiar feeling of a looming loss of innocence. My *realist* mind understood. In a high-stakes competition where a lot of money is at stake, people constantly try to deceive others. Case in point: a deal. Deception can take many forms, but it's often skirting ethics. You portray information in a non-intuitive way in order to hide things; you avoid questions; you listen selectively. Each time this happened, with each "little white lie" my inner idealism suffered another of a thousand small paper cuts, like a small part of me was dying.

There are plenty of amazing people inside the capital markets system, like Scott Burns. But how in the hell are we supposed to feel human when the control room of the entire system *rewards* hyper-competitive gorillas like Dick Fuld and Roe Stamps, men led by their fear of losing? It's no wonder virtually everyone inside the system ends up with a protective persona. It's perilous as shit in there and have to don that armor to protect yourself.

Or do you?

At some point, we all face a choice: do we keep slipping down into the belly of the white-sheep world, or do we say "fuck it" and do things a bit differently?

Whenever I meet a "deal guy" these days, I can pretty much guarantee that I'm going to be interacting with their ego or some persona, and I completely understand why. Damn right it's hard to be human while living inside systems where almost every incentive rewards us for *not* being human. There's a reason why pretty much everyone inside the white-sheep world, including Leon Black, loses track of their inner child and their inner artist. The moment you're vulnerable or too human, someone may try to screw you over. You might be exposed as the imposter you think you really are, down deep. You might *fail*. As Roe Stamps IV understood, there are a few things that every insecure overachiever fears, and the most devastating of those things is being a *loser*.

Oh, man.

⚡

Aunt Liz's and Uncle Joe's high school—our high school—sits in a lush basin surrounded by a thicket of pine trees, just over a ridge from the town of Colfax, California. It's so peaceful and quiet at first light and at dusk that deer sometimes graze on the school's soccer field. Nestled in the foothills of the Sierra Nevada Mountains, between Sacramento and Lake Tahoe, Colfax is one of the many small towns that were built up during the California Gold Rush. With a population of just under 2,000 people, the downtown had no stoplights, aside from the railroad crossing at the crux of town, and Main Street hadn't changed all that much since the late 1800s. This was rural America—what would become Trump country.

When you grow up or live in rural America, the rest of the world mostly comes to you, or it doesn't. You never feel

like you really know the "big world" out there—places like
New York, London, or even San Francisco, just a few hours
away. You know your town well—usually too well. You know
first names; you know backstories; you know the gossip. The
rest of the world is mostly an abstraction, appearing only in
faraway glimpses. Or interactions measured in minutes. City
folk pull off for gas, a burger, or snacks—their Cadillacs, Beem-
ers, or Audis draped with ski racks. They drive fast, move fast,
talk fast, and eat fast. City folks always seemed to move with a
certain sense of confidence or even arrogance—like they knew
something you didn't. You couldn't help but feel a bit intimi-
dated, or occasionally harassed.

"Flatlanders!" Uncle Joe called them for a while, before shifting to "Cidiots!"

If a cidiot drove too closely behind his truck, he would say,
"Eat my stinger; I don't care!" He was referring to the logging truck
hitch that extended from the back of the trailer when it was empty.

It was in the solitude of the deep woods where Uncle Joe felt
at home and most deeply alive. His father had been a logger, and
his son Nick would become one. Being out in the woods, out in
nature, was deeply etched into their souls and spirits; there was
no other way to be.

I never once heard Uncle Joe complain about work or getting up so early to do it. Not once. Nor did he groan about his
health, even as his body deteriorated. He did, however, have
choice words for politicians and hedge-fund managers, who he
often called "money whores." And he certainly agreed with The
Notorious B.I.G.: mo' money led to mo' problems.

When Uncle Joe and Aunt Liz were visiting London and I
showed them our offices at Clifford Street, in the posh fashion

district of Mayfair in London, they marveled at it all. As Uncle Joe kept snapping all kinds of photos, he kept telling me that I was (now) his "retirement plan." It was a proud moment in many ways, yet it was also one of those interesting moments in life when two vastly different worlds collided.

My head was still in the white-sheep world, but my heart was with Uncle Joe. It was less than a year later that I left my job, but at that time I still wasn't ready to leave the white-sheep world.

CHAPTER SIX

VIEW FROM THE TOP

fter leaving London, Summit, and the capital markets, I
went to business school to try to figure out what to do
with my life. At school, I heard Bill George, the former
CEO of Medtronic turned Harvard Business School Professor,
speak one day. He talked a lot about authentic leadership, and
his words resonated. You are most effective as a leader, he argued,
when you are yourself, not some persona. After serendipitously
meeting Bill later that day as he toured campus, we became pen
pals. He would ask for my feedback on his ideas and we learned
a lot from the exchanges, so much so that Bill asked if I would be
interested in co-authoring the book *True North: Discover Your
Authentic Leadership*. I enthusiastically signed on and entered
another portal into the inner-workings of the power structure of
the white-sheep world. We ultimately interviewed 125 leaders
of all ages, including dozens of CEOs of large companies—from
eBay to Starbucks to Novartis to Charles Schwab.

Peering inside life at the top of big companies unveiled more of the pitfalls and punishments inside the system. There's a certain irony at the top of the white-sheep world. These are all still people with the same human needs as you and I. They too want close relationships, intimate connection, and to feel belonging. Many CEOs, not surprisingly, are sensitive and dislike conflict, and seek to avoid it at all costs. After all, part of their success has come from not having offended too many people, so that there aren't too many negative voices in the ears of the board of directors choosing the next CEO. In order to get to the top, most CEOs have spent their whole lives in a system that rewards them for spending a large part of their lives in fear and some type of protective persona. It's indescribably hard. Preserving their humanity requires heroic effort, especially in such a lonely fishbowl surrounded by white sheep.

Now, I want to again emphasize that my use of terms like "the white-sheep world" are simply metaphors to describe a system that controls many of our lives at one point or another. Even in the spirit of play and fun and "ha ha ha" that my inner child resorts to when poking fun at my years in the white-sheep world, my wiser self recognizes that I put myself in danger of being "cancelled," taken out by a sniper, or sued by various white-sheep groups. Devout bastions of white sheepism *might* include the NFL owners; the DMV; your local towing company; Harvard Business School; the League of Shadows; Washington, DC; or Goldman Sachs. (I use the term "might" since the white-sheep world thrives on the literal and the legal.)

Being CEO of Goldman Sachs is one of the most sought-after positions in the white-sheep world. Lloyd Blankfein concluded a relentless rise to the top when he became CEO of Goldman in

2006, having started on Wall Street as a trader decades before. Blankfein was openly irritated in the 2010s, some say angry, when following the Global Financial Crisis and the accompanying hits to Goldman's reputation, Blankfein was shown chart after chart about why the firm had been losing so much ground in getting top talent. Blankfein was particularly exasperated by the charts because he told everyone how Goldman kept getting harder and harder to get into. That's only because the denominator (the applicants) was increasing, he was told. The quality of the numerator (the candidates) was decreasing.

Oh, man.

An important reason for why Goldman was losing out on high-quality talent was that the "cooler" side of the career tracks through the 2010s had become the world of entrepreneurship. The good news as far as I was concerned was that as the decade passed, the black sheep of New York City retained an increasing amount of territory across the greater five boroughs, even if Manhattan remained firmly in the hands of white sheep. Naturally, plenty of insecure overachievers were drawn to these bastions of "prestige" like Goldman Sachs, a carefully marketed, self-reinforcing idea that works very well as an organizing principle for your life until something cooler comes along.

Speaking of something cooler coming along, Blankfein was CEO for twelve years, until he passed the reins to a DJ. That sentence makes me giggle just writing it, as does an imaginary *New York Post* headline: *DJ Promoted to CEO of Goldman Sachs*. Well, actually, Blankfein's heir as Goldman CEO, David Solomon, is very much an amateur DJ. But when I learned about Solomon's alter ego performing under the name "DJ D-Sol," I was captivated. If a black sheep had taken over as CEO at

Goldman Sachs, that would represent a major coup, like the revolutionaries taking Fort Ticonderoga from the Brits in 1775 at the outset of the Revolutionary War. The idealization was short-lived, however.

I'm not saying that David Solomon isn't a black sheep at heart. We all have a creative side, buried or hidden as it can be, and I loved that he was unleashing and expressing his.

I'm just saying that if you want to become CEO of a company like Goldman Sachs, close to the center of the matrix, you have to master the dark arts of the hierarchical (and patriarchal) white-sheep world. There aren't many black sheep in the corridors or boardrooms of Fortune 500 companies. Strong egos and personas get rewarded. Once you get to the top levels of these organizations, especially a place like Goldman Sachs, you naturally have to navigate a *Game of Thrones*-like gauntlet of power. You must quickly see through people, including their skills and motives, in order to determine if they are a friend or foe. You have to be ruthless about this and seek out the right allies while constantly watching your back. If you don't have a killer instinct, capable of eliminating threats, people will see that and immediately discount you or use you. It's not a context that rewards living according to spiritual mindsets, such as "we are all one," very much.

You learn when you're young to become much more strategic as you ascend in the white-sheep world because that's how you win. You might even take a class in business school called Paths to Power, as I did, where the central messages are about how to be more strategic, and how the world isn't fair. You learn that people who get into positions of power learn how to self-promote, network, and focus like a laser on acquiring the right allies. Hard work is table stakes for getting to the top. You are taught that if you want to be a CEO of a big company, you must learn a whole new mindset, such as how to use flattery and feign intimacy effectively. You are shown videos of Bill Clinton creating intimacy by shaking hands with one hand while holding the upper shoulder of the person with the other. You are taught the white-sheep playbook on how to spend a life transacting with endless transactional people seeking intimacy on your path to power. At the top of the white-sheep world, everyone is basically using everybody else, while also living with the persistent fear of being used.

But wait: the gauntlet to the corner office doesn't end there. After you've learned how to manage threats, create the right alliances, and position yourself for the top job, the last requirement is to control risks. You've spent your whole life getting to this place, and there is no turning back now. Sure, it's lonely at the top. You would be too, in a context where virtually every interaction is transactional and every day features countless gestures of false intimacy. It's the intimacy you've had to trade off in life every day in which you've made the choice to advance your career. You are lucky if you experience a genuine, deep, intimate bond with your spouse. You are also lucky if you have a handful of close, real friendships in life with people who have no business interests in you, and who see you for the essence of who you really are. You don't really trust many people, which means you don't have many real friends. Oh—one more thing: the moment you are no longer CEO, people will stop calling, and all those people and transactional relationships will go away.

Not quite what I would have expected from afar, and worthy of some real compassion, even if the CEO is a total asshole, which would likely trace back to some deep traumas.

Now, are you actually happy once you make it to the top? Some days you are; some days you aren't. Mostly it's stressful. You have about a thousand potential decisions swirling in your mind: some large choices like what to do in China; some smaller, like worrying about that *New York Times* story you know is in the works. If you're a world-class CEO, you're like a general, whirring from one topic and person to the next, especially if you care about getting to the core of things. Some CEOs mostly want to go to Davos and spend time with prime ministers and presidents, while the best get into the nitty gritty and drive change. Your family doesn't really get to experience you when you're the CEO of a big company; nor do your real friends. It's a completely soul-engulfing job that really is lonely. You always have to think about what Wall Street wants and ask yourself all the time if any email you send might one day be subpoenaed and used to embarrass or prosecute you.

I don't care what anyone says; it's not a job that allows you to really *live*, so why are jobs (and lives) like these aspirational for so many who dream of "success"?

There are naturally some great parts of being a CEO. The world mostly revolves around your needs and desires inside the company, so you'll get ego hits every day and can make things happen. People accord you respect both inside and outside the company. Bono might even reach out to you to partner on something. If your company is relevant enough, you'll regularly meet celebrities and snap pictures with them, which you hope (and subconsciously believe) will make your kids think you're cool. That's a very important motivator to any CEO or investor, by the way: they want their kids to think they're cool. Alas, CEOs are rarely cool, especially when compared with artistic types like Bono, but being cool is an aspiration for many CEOs, beyond the title.

That brings us back to Goldman Sachs and David Solomon. Now, according to our Black Sheep informants inside Goldman Sachs, what David Solomon wants more than money, power, and even status is to be *cool*. That helps explain his alter ego. Outside his day job, DJ D-Sol usually wears black t-shirts and silver headphones and can be seen spinning on his Pioneer system, including at Hamptons parties or bars in the Bahamas. Objectively speaking, you might find his music underwhelming, including a remix of Fleetwood Mac's *Don't Stop* and Fontella Bass's *Rescue Me*, although it got better by 2021 when he released a song with Ryan Tedder of OneRepublic.

But, encouragingly, music brings Solomon alive. "It's a lot of fun. I get real joy when I'm DJ'ing," he told podcast host Nic Harcourt. "It's joyful in a way that's very hard to describe."

When I found out that Solomon had been listed on the docket for Lollapalooza Chicago in 2022, my inner smartass compelled me to email him to ask if he had paid for the performance slot. His response was endearing, saying that the shocking thing was that *they* would pay *him* (the proceeds of which he would pass on to his mental health charity). "Should be amazing even though I am sure i (sic) am on the smallest stage there!" he enthused, perhaps providing a small window into his inner child.

After spending his professional life in suits and navigating the *Game of Thrones* white-sheep world, being a DJ is where Solomon's inner artist can come out to play. In my mind, Solomon would be truly successful only if he's living his best life, full of joy—yet somehow that's not our cultural norm.

Solomon is interesting as an illustration of the gravitational pull of the white-sheep world versus the black-sheep world. Somehow, success (in the white-sheep world at least) has come to mean that you're really good at living in a persona to win at an artificial game, where money, titles, and social status are the prize. Solomon attained an ultimate prize as CEO of Goldman, and you can be sure that if the Goldman Board of Directors told him to stop DJ'ing in order to be CEO, he would quit. The white-sheep world doesn't give a damn what Solomon's inner child might have to say about anything. Joy isn't a metric in capitalism; nor are any other measures of well-being.

We become what we measure, and we currently live in a system that is driven predominantly by fear: the fear of losing that which can be measured, even if we've lost ourselves in the process. Only the lucky ones like Scott Burns even realize what life is possible on the other side of the matrix.

So many of us have long traded off deeper fulfillment and happiness, especially when everyone thinks of you as "successful." There are some simple psychological explanations for why. We know from the research on "loss aversion," for one, that the pain of losing $100 is psychologically twice as powerful for humans as the pleasure of gaining $100. My heart wrenches knowing that the fear of losing money, title, or status is far more powerful than the joy of gaining more joy or happiness. This is the ultimate tragedy of living life according to the rules and success metrics of the white-sheep world.

That brings me back to the far bigger question: why the hell do we live in a world dominated by this inhumane system of success?

It took years for me to really understand how and why the consensus view of the purpose of business became *make money*. Yes; a bunch of economists and academics like Milton Friedman won an intellectual argument dating back to the 1970s, when he argued: "There is one and only one social responsibility of business—to use its resources and engage in activities designed to increase its profits." But most of the time, what academics say goes ignored. No; the real problem is when other people say, "It's the law!" That is, it's the law that if you're an executive or on the board of a company, you are required to serve the shareholders' interests above everything else.

About 66% of the Fortune 500 companies based in the United States are incorporated in Delaware. That is why it mattered profoundly when the former Chief Justice of the Delaware Supreme Court, Leo Strine, took a firm stand supporting shareholder primacy over all other stakeholders during his tenure. Strine in 2015:

> [A] clear-eyed look at the law of corporations
> in Delaware reveals that, within the limits of
> their discretion, directors must make stockholder
> welfare their sole end, and that other interests
> may be taken into consideration only as a means
> of promoting stockholder welfare.

If you were to ask me about what is crushing human souls and the environment, not to mention innovation, more than any other idea (aside from certain dictatorships), the idea of shareholder primacy would be it.

Even Judge Strine changed his tune, acknowledging by 2021 that companies and investors were "starting to feel the simmering boil of discontent." What's more, he conceded, "we created a world trading system in which we didn't embed environmental or labor protections."

Actually, what we created is an inhumane world run by inhumane systems. The mounting costs are visible to everyone, shared by almost everyone, and awaiting . . . *something*.

Luckily, none of the systems arrayed against us are set in stone. It is small groups of people acting together, all of us, not CEOs, that actually change things. Talent preferences and values change, for one. Consumer preferences change. The matrix of the capital markets, even, is held together by only a sinew of psychology: our shared belief and trust in that system. But if we don't even know another framework for success or what's possible for living in an entirely different mindset, little will change.

In order to find another path, I needed to spend time with the happiest person I knew. And I needed to find Gandalf.

CHAPTER SEVEN

THE WISE SHEEP

A fter working with all kinds of people deemed successful by society who seemed chronically unfulfilled in the
white-sheep world, it struck me that the happiest person
I knew was my mother. If there was a true black sheep in our
family, it was Mom. She came from a family of artists: her mother
and brother were artists, and before having children, Mom was a
photographer. Living in the San Francisco Bay area in the 1960s
and 70s, she wasn't a hippie so much as an observer of history
unfolding. She got in with a hip crowd and photographed a
bunch of interesting people including Ken Kesey and some of his
fellow Merry Pranksters, who Tom Wolfe chronicled in *The Electric Kool-Aid Acid Test.* The Merry Pranksters were surely black
sheep, and their bus tour inspired ours to some extent, although
their values were more exhibitionist than the "we" values of
our crew. Mom also photographed George Lucas at his house

after *American Graffiti* came out, back when Lucas was writing *Star Wars* and had a copy of Joseph Campbell's *The Hero with a Thousand Faces* sitting on his desk. Mom always seemed to have had her finger on the pulse of the cultural zeitgeist. One of the San Francisco papers even named her one of the city's Most Eligible Bachelorettes.

After Dad got appointed to the Superior Court in our rural county when I was three, Mom became the only practicing Buddhist I knew. She picked up spiritual practice in her mid-30s, feeling a lack of fulfillment and the demands of two young children. She practiced diligently: every day she meditated for about an hour; she also practiced yoga. She read dozens of books about Buddhism, filling an entire bookshelf, and attended retreats once or twice a year. I'm not going to lie: I thought it was all a bit weird at times, since I was mostly focused on sports. I mean, she had an orange Free Tibet sticker on the rear bumper of her car. And sometimes she made us memorize quotes from the Dalai Lama as a disciplinary measure. Who does that? Once she took my brother and me to a daylong retreat with some Buddhist named Thich Nhat Hanh. We even went for a little hike with him (and dozens of other people). Only later did I realize that Thich Nhat Hanh was one of the most enlightened spiritual leaders of his generation.

"We are here to awaken from our illusion of separateness," Nhat Hanh had said. It was a phrase that illustrated how Mom lived.

Following my parents' courteous divorce while I was in London, a tacit acknowledgement of different desired paths, Mom found her way to the coast and a houseboat-oasis. Mom's houseboat in Sausalito is a small, two-story house on a floating foundation, surrounded by swimming seals and all kinds of birds, the tides ebbing and flowing. Called The Dragon's Teahouse, the boat has an Asian vibe, including a red-and-brown color scheme.

I was determined to make my way to the other side of the matrix, but I couldn't work out how. Mom had made it. Her secret to being so genuinely fulfilled, it seemed, was that she didn't live in ideas of who she was. She lived in her essence; Mom just *was*. She took joy in nature, following her curiosities, and always her relationships and her family. She had nothing to prove. She was just *connected*—with herself, with others, and with nature.

It's amazing how much we overcomplicate our lives when the simplest mindsets lead to the greatest fulfillment.

When I first ventured out of the matrix, I spent countless months and years even, feeling completely lost, yet she constantly encouraged me by saying things would eventually come together. I wasn't nearly as certain, and the self-doubt felt crippling at times. While most of my classmates from business school and the rest of the world worked in jobs, I was going on long walks with my mom. This went on for months. I felt so lost, all I could do (in life) was put one foot in front of the other. I was in a cocoon, hiding from the world, going through some type of metamorphosis; a triple bypass of identity change.

"You'll figure it out," she'd say often and with complete confidence.

Through the crucible of darkness and despair, I came to understand just how profoundly Mom's spiritual essence influenced me. When the shit hit the fan, not only did I retreat to the houseboat for peace; I also read some of her Buddhism books, including ones by the well-known teacher Pema Chödrön, such as *When Things Fall Apart*. Chödrön was Mom's spiritual mentor and they were friends; Mom even transcribed one or two of her books.

"Whatever it takes," Mom would say, referring to the many spiritual paths people travel to find themselves.

As I unwrapped the layers of my constructed identity like a mummy, I learned that the world ultimately wants our energy, our talents, and our essence. Mom's essence was very calm and low-drama, and she exuded kindness like the Dalai Lama. People were drawn to her for these reasons, and because she seemed to be living her best life. She didn't need validation or affirmation from anyone. It made me think a lot about how in the Western world we spend way too much time in our heads and identities, rather than our bodies, just living. Perhaps, I imagined, the world would one day better balance the rationalism of the Western world with the deep wisdom of the Asian world, and be a lot happier.

The joy of living a full and inspired life that Mom had found through her spiritual practices, relationships, and curiosities wasn't what my classmates from the Stanford Graduate School of Business talked about. Obsessing about careers was the norm, and such a boring fucking topic, if you think about it. I'd rather go to the Westminster Kennel Club Dog Show with Scott Burns and watch a bunch of prima-donna dogs and their owners prance around. That was living, as far as I was concerned; something memorable, at least. I was astounded to see at our reunions that only a handful of people out of our class of roughly 390 seem genuinely and completely fulfilled with their lives and careers. A few classmates had "made it big" in conventional MBA success terms: two co-founded an online real-estate company that was acquired for over $3 billion; another was reportedly paid $100 million *not* to leave Google; others made a lot of money as investors. Relatively speaking, most felt like they hadn't accomplished much, or even gotten pointed in the right direction yet. Now, if a person can't be happy as a Stanford business school graduate living on an upper-middle-class income or more, there is a far larger failure in the system.

Crazy, right?

One explanation: our educational institutions have largely failed to create cultures that support us in finding and cultivating true sources of joy, fulfillment, and well-being. Although it's very good to see more diversity of voices at Stanford Business now than when I was a student, what got elevated and celebrated back then were the people who made it to the top or made a lot of money. Steve Jobs. CEOs. Founders who built valuable companies like Mark Zuckerberg. Wealthy investors. Ed Catmull, sure, but Ed Catmull the Pixar founder, not Ed Catmull the Buddhist. The atmosphere promotes persistent "upward comparison" by celebrating a narrow definition of success, which leads to burnout and unhappiness.

Make no mistake: it's very hard to eject from that matrix.

During the time I stayed with Mom, I drove to a nearby theater to watch *Into the Wild*, a movie based on the story of Christopher McCandless (played by Emile Hirsch), a young man who was trying to find an authentic path in life. The quest ultimately took McCandless deep into the wilds of Alaska, where he found an abandoned bus, which he named The Magic Bus, and found genuine happiness in nature (at least for a while). On his journey, one scene struck me especially, and I was surprised to find myself crying. In the scene, Hirsch drives through a city when he sees a group of people dressed in suits, enjoying happy hour. Hirsch's expression conveys feelings of loss, as if grieving for the life he has left behind, as he heads towards an uncertain future.

In that scene, that character was me. It's just so damn hard, I thought at that moment, as emotion welled up inside, and tears started to stream down my cheeks in the darkened theater. It's just so damn hard to be original in this life. It's so damn hard to walk away from what others deem "successful," especially when the tradeoffs are so real. That guy in the suit talking with the beautiful women had been me in London, and probably still could have been me if I would only take a conventional path. I could have stayed in venture capital on the partner track, I thought in my moments of greatest doubt. But I knew I couldn't turn back. My girlfriend's family was deeply concerned about my lack of direction and consequently for their daughter. She (and they) wanted a "white picket fence" life for us, while I was being pulled towards a more creative path. Our relationship would come to an end, and I would lose about twenty-five pounds.

Mom never seemed to worry about my struggle, at least outwardly. She didn't value those traditional forms of success, and that was the perspective I needed.

"To thine own self be true," she had frequently told me when I was a boy, and I was resolved to do so. I didn't feel like I had any other choice. As my mother's son, I was appropriately becoming a black sheep.

꙳

It was one of those rare sunny mornings in San Francisco, uncomplicated by fog. After walking across Lafayette Park towards the bay, I savored the view, which included Alcatraz a couple of miles off in the distance. It was about 8:15 a.m. as I walked down Octavia Street, one of the city's famously-steep streets, towards my gym on Union Street, about six blocks away. Nearing the end of the first block, at the steepest descent, an older man was walking up towards me.

"Wait. Is that . . . ?" I wondered. "Nah . . . it couldn't be."

Wait. Holy shit! It definitely was Ed Catmull.

Like Gandalf, Catmull possessed great wisdom, and was a bit of a hermit.

"Ed?!" I blurted out with a guttural, enthusiastic life-force.

Calmly, Ed stopped on the sidewalk, looked up and held his hand to the sunlight in order to see up the hill.

"Oh—hey, Peter," he said, his tone matter-of-fact, one hand waving while the other was taking off his headphones.

I couldn't believe my eyes. Just a few blocks from my apartment, I had stumbled across Ed Catmull. Looking nothing like a CEO, he was all sweaty and dressed in full workout attire, including a red headband and fingerless weightlifting gloves.

"Wait—are you coming from Crunch?" I asked, trying to hold back my disbelief that Ed Catmull would use the same, fairly plain-Jane, inexpensive gym as I, especially with an Equinox just down the street.

"Yep. Three mornings a week," he replied, to my joy.

"So you *live* here?" I emphasized, trying to piece it all together.

"Yes. We live over on Pacific," he replied with zero pretense, calmly pointing over to his right. Still damp from the gym, he reminded me of a kindly uncle or relative behind his wire-framed specs and salt-and-pepper beard.

Except—holy shit—Ed Catmull was my neighbor. The visionary and co-founder of Pixar, and, hell, just a creative force, the Gandalf of the digitally-animated movie space, was my *neighbor.*

Running into Catmull in the Pixar parking lot the day the Black Sheep idea came to me wasn't the first time I'd encountered him. I had met him when he gave a lecture at the Stanford computer science department and I offered to send him some feedback on it. Catmull encouraged people to speak honestly about problems they saw at Pixar, so he welcomed my offer and handed me his assistant's card. That is how I came to write the MEMO TO ED.

As I penned my thoughts back then, it was a big commitment to spend a day on a side project, let alone two days. Although I wasn't quite living on Ramen at the time, I was counting my dimes and dollars. But something inside me kept urging me on and to do my best work. I had read everything I could possibly get my hands on about Ed Catmull and the creation of Pixar, and was endlessly captivated. It was an incredible tale of an unlikely cast of misfits bringing an impossible dream to life.

Well, that memo was the best freaking memo I've ever written: seven or eight pages, footnoted and everything. I didn't expect I'd ever talk with him again, but our paths just kept crossing. First in the Pixar parking lot, and now this. I took it all as a sign. Of what, I had no idea yet.

By that morning, I could sleep a bit easier because my second book, *Little Bets*, had come out and was a success. But I was still in the early stages of figuring out what the Black Sheep tribe might evolve into. Like Ed did in his 30s in starting Pixar, I had stepped into the vast unknown and was still completely unsure of what it might become. I sketched out my big dream and vision for Black Sheep on a sheet of paper. Across the top of the page, I wrote "BLK SHP Vision: To help advance a new era of American enlightenment, deeply engaged and willing to lock arms in collaboration with brothers & sisters from all races, religions, and sexual orientations to help catalyze a renaissance of creativity, entrepreneurship, invention, and innovation . . ."

That was the audacious dream. Beneath that wording, I sketched out the elements that I believed would be needed to accomplish such a thing. It included Black-Sheep-branded businesses to fund the whole effort, a thought-leadership and publishing platform, and BLK SHP communities around the world. While I realized back then that the dream was close to impossible, the one person and group I had known to accomplish something similarly audacious was Ed Catmull and his colleagues at Pixar. Thus, crossing paths with Gandalf again was timely.

Sure, he lived in a Victorian house with Academy Awards on the mantle while I was renting a junior one-bedroom, but we lived about four blocks apart. And when I showed up at the gym and hopped on the elliptical machine, there, every other day or so, was Ed on an elliptical machine right in front of me. No one else in the gym had the slightest idea who he was.

From the start, Ed embraced the Black Sheep ethos, including our audacious dream, happily wearing the hat. Turns out he always saw himself as the black sheep of his family, so instead of becoming an educator like everyone else, he found his calling as a computer scientist focused on digital animation. During work for his Ph.D. at the University of Utah in 1972, where he studied with Alan Kay, who years later would point Steve Jobs to Pixar, Ed had created a one-minute, digitally-animated short film of his left hand called *A Computer Animated Hand*. It was considered revolutionary, and it became a precursor to the whole field of digital animation. From those days in the early 1970s, Ed had a dream: to make art, which to him meant to make the first full-length, digitally-animated film.

People thought Catmull and his crew were crazy because the technology to make a digitally-animated film was seen to be decades off. Undeterred, Ed ended up running Lucasfilm's computer graphics arm, later renamed Pixar, and the company spent the early years developing the technology to support digital animation. Pixar began its life as a hardware company focused on high-end digital imagery.

Steve Jobs believed in their technology and talent, so in 1986 he bought Pixar, still a hardware company, from George Lucas for $5 million. The timing was right. Lucas was going through a costly divorce and Jobs had recently been ousted from Apple. Ed's quest ultimately took ten years more than he anticipated, but by the time *Toy Story* came out in 1995, the first full-length, digitally-animated film, they had invented a new industry.

Pretty much everyone at Pixar in those early days was a black sheep. There was Alvy Ray Smith, a genius graphics technologist who was such a maverick that he eventually told Steve Jobs to go to hell (in so many words) and left the company. There was also John Lasseter, the former Disney animator who had been fired from Disney mostly for insubordination. His new job was to make short films to demonstrate the value of Pixar's hardware. Lasseter would spearhead the production of a new digitally-animated short film each year despite intense criticism from many people in the company who couldn't understand why a hardware-turned-software company was so spiritually focused on short films. But to Ed, John, and company, selling hardware was always just a means to an end. They came to see Steve Jobs as their protector.

Jobs ultimately invested about $50 million of his own money into Pixar. He also tried to sell the company multiple times, in hopes of just breaking even. Luckily for him and everyone at Pixar, he didn't sell the company, because in one of the most unlikely stories of modern business, Pixar's first digitally-animated film, *Toy Story*, earned over $300 million. Eventually, Disney acquired Pixar for $7.4 billion in 2006, making Steve Jobs Disney's largest shareholder. Back at Pixar, the motley crew of misfits had done it, despite all odds. None of them individually could have done it. Together, however, they changed the world. It ended up taking twenty years, but *they fucking did it.*

Talk about black sheep.

Having Ed just a few blocks away kept things in perspective. Oftentimes he would get off his elliptical machine, notice me, and come over to say hello.

"How's it all going?" he asked one morning when I felt particularly insecure.

"Uh . . . We're making progress and having fun," I replied tentatively, since my friends and I were experimenting like crazy on this Black Sheep idea, trying to figure out what to do with it.

"Well, having fun is the most important thing," he offered before turning towards the stairs to walk up to the weight room. The comment would have seemed cliché coming from most people. From Ed it was gold. Ed had publicly and repeatedly risked everything to make Pixar what he felt it had to be, which was a place where fun was an important thing. In that moment, his encouragement meant the world.

One morning, I walked upstairs and saw Ed was the only person on the floor. There he was across the room from me, lying on a bench, holding a bar loaded with weights. Suddenly, he started a set, lifting and grunting. And I mean *really grunting*, as if he was a weightlifter at the Olympics. The whole scene made an impression. For such a calm, kind, and reserved man, it was the first time I had seen the caged animal inside him, a bit of his own inner-Sulley.

"Wow!" I thought. All that drive and determination that it took to invent a new industry was starting to make sense. Seeing Ed in the gym was a bit like watching a caged animal be released.

Mornings at the gym turned out to be just the beginning. Before long, Ed and I developed a playful banter like a couple of kids. We'd go on walks around the neighborhood and just talk. Well, mostly Ed talked and I listened. He had a story about everything, and liked to go down rabbit holes. Stories about family. Stories about building culture. Stories about how toy-manufacturing lead times could be shortened. Stories about some dumb-shit decision someone made. Lots of stories about Steve Jobs, with whom Ed worked for 26 years after Jobs bought Pixar. Stories about why two teams doing roughly the same thing can perform so differently. It was a master class on innovation and life, wrapped around lots of laughter and joking, probably because our inner children turned out to be around the same age.

Ed's inner child is about four years old. "Four years old *at best*," he would say when the topic came up.

When asked, people usually have an intuition about the age of their inner child. Mine is about seven years old, playful as the day is long. That was the age when my second-grade teacher, Ms. Welch, kept bombarding us with worksheet after worksheet. It was boring. I was restless. I just wanted to play, so I would constantly ask to go to the bathroom. Ms. Welch grew tired of the routine and my attitude in general, so she kicked me out of the advanced class the next year. Separated from my friends and wondering why, it marked an end of my childhood innocence, which seems like a marker of sorts for where our inner child age might also reside. Even as I type this, there's a big part of me that just wants to get out and *play*.

Since my inner child is slightly older than Ed's, I offered that my inner child could mentor his. He liked that. It was kind of like the Karate Kid offering to mentor Mr. Miyagi. Now, if I had said something like that to Scott Collins back in London, he would have looked like he wanted to kick my ass. When those piercing blue "linebacker's eyes" blazed at me, my inner child would retreat into the depths of my soul. Collins didn't really seem to have an inner child, or if he did, it came across like an ever-responsible teenager, while Scott Burns' inner child seemed about five or six years old.

Collins frequently seemed *too* responsible. You know the type. He would often ask me why I was laughing or "What is so funny?" I can remember the first time it happened. About four months after I joined the firm as an Associate, I was in the hallway of the Boston office. Collins rounded the corner, walking purposefully with his head down when, all of a sudden, he just stopped and looked at the ground for about ten seconds before he pivoted and went back to his office. It was a really goofy looking, awkward pause, so I started laughing. It was noticeable enough that he asked me what was so funny, and I replied, "Your mannerisms." Well, that was not the type of thing Associates usually told Partners, and he didn't think that was so funny.

The main piece of feedback Collins had for me was delivered during my first year in London. One night, we decided to have a bowling outing with our small-yet-growing six-person team. On the way to the bowling alley, I got in the elevator as Collins held the door open and we waited for our colleague Sotiris, who as usual couldn't get his shit together. After a minute or two, Collins, still dressed in his suit and tie, got that look again, like he was about to blow a gasket. All I could think was "we're going *bowling*. I mean, what's the rush? We're not closing a deal; we're going off to have *fun*, right?" And, well, a giggle just slipped out. I couldn't contain it.

In a nanosecond, all of Collins' intensity and palpably aggressive steely eyes went from being focused on Sotiris to being focused on me. "You know," he said with a growl as he let the elevator close. "You really need to work on not laughing at inappropriate times."

Back then, I thought he was completely right. He was the adult in the room, the whiter sheep who was giving me a piece of feedback to chew on. If he spied it, I did have a problem. However, with the benefit of hindsight, I think that he may have been the one who had the problem, as does anyone else who takes themselves too seriously. And taking yourself too seriously might be a good indicator that you've lost touch with your inner child. I mean, especially when you're going *bowling*. Scott Collins needed Scott Burns and me for a reason: we could remind him that he had an inner child.

I can remember one Monday night when Collins and I worked until midnight. He offered me a ride home. Behind the wheel of his Mercedes station wagon, he started asking me all these questions about which way we should be going. Since I mostly took the Tube and routinely got lost on London's streets, I was clueless. So there he was trying to predict what directions the streets were going in, how to beat the traffic lights, and whatnot. His mood vacillated between intense and joking. We got to one red light and he said, "Oh, we're fucked!" He was serious. I started laughing; I just couldn't help it. Then he started to mimic my old boss back in Boston, Marty Mannion, saying, "Pete, . . . we're *fucked.*" That playful sense of humor that made him so endearing had crept out. We both started laughing and giggling like a couple six-year-olds. Call it our *Big Lebowski* moment—a beautiful moment of connection.

It took me years of wandering and wondering to puzzle this through, and what I came to understand is if we equate success with happiness, part of being a successful adult means getting to know and embracing our inner child. Do that and we'd all be a lot happier. Consider one significant example that Mom helped me discover: the Dalai Lama shared a deep kinship and decades of laughs and joy with Desmond Tutu and the two men having bonded over their inner (roughly) five-year-olds. In inner-child, playful, "flow" realms, I learned, our brains are producing an enhanced neurochemical state, including a rise in dopamine, serotonin, and endorphins. In such states, we are experiencing a more innocent, child-like version of ourselves, and don't need anything else to be fulfilled or happy.

Being easily entertained by life is, therefore, a talent. I could spend all day coming up with nicknames for people. Scott Collins, for instance, resembled Buzz Lightyear in more ways than one: from his protruded jaw to taking himself a bit too seriously at times." "You're mocking me, aren't you?" Buzz said to Woody in *Toy Story*. Meanwhile, the most important thing I learned from all those days at the gym and our walks and conversations was that Ed was just a human being, just like you and me. Although he was quite driven, which was obvious at the gym and in his life, he didn't live in his ego or in some invited persona. He never wanted to be anything but Ed—just a regular person, nothing special. His rare humility and lack of ego led to a nickname. Someone mentioned one day that people around Pixar, including Brad Bird, called Ed "The Pope."

"And I'm not even Catholic," Ed would dead-pan, since he was a practicing Buddhist.

It has been decades since Leon Black and Ed Catmull were young Jedis. Black went on to conquer Wall Street and became a lot wealthier than Catmull or almost anyone else in their generation. But was he really successful? Catmull, on the other hand, assembled a rebel alliance of black sheep who changed the world, eventually touching the inner child of billions of people with Pixar's films.

One night over dinner years later, after we became good friends and colleagues as advisors at Google's semi-secret innovation laboratory, I asked Ed if he felt particularly proud of his and Pixar's positive impact on humanity, especially when it's so rare for a corporation to have such a human ethos.

"I don't think about that very much," he replied. "I'm most proud when people at Pixar can uncover and solve problems on their own."

That was Ed in a nutshell: the journey was the reward. His practice was mindfulness and meditation. Sure enough, Ed Catmull was the first Buddhist Pope.

CHAPTER EIGHT

STAGING AN INSURGENCY

New York City was fertile ground for rounding up black sheep to join in our newborn quest. While Manhattan was surely a prime white-sheep pasture, Brooklyn was a black-sheep haven. Those two worlds always seemed to want to come together. The city has 21 bridges and 15 tunnels, yet clans ranging from Wu-Tang to Wall Street rarely meet, unless it's in the subway or Yankee Stadium. I mean, if Manhattan and Brooklyn could just have sex, it seemed like the city would be so much happier. The bankers and commercial types always wanted to hang out with the artists, the designers, and musicians and have a few drinks and maybe a joint. Pretty much everyone needs to let go of their social identities and anxieties—if only for a minute—and be human.

At the launch event of the New York Black Sheep, the worlds collided for a few hours one rainy December night in the basement of the Ace Hotel, just off Broadway on 29th. Questlove, the legendary DJ and drummer and leader of The Roots,leaned over two turntables, preparing for his set. He rarely looked up or made eye contact, yet sensed the crowd and the room. Wearing thick, red-framed glasses with a trademark Afro pick sticking out of his expansive bushy hair atop his 6'4" frame, he put on his silver-rimmed headphones and queued up the first song, George Clinton's *We Want the Funk*.

The shit was on.

The room was Questlove's kind of room: a mosaic of the city's five boroughs, pulsating with energy and diversity. A fire dancer from Harlem. Designers, photographers, and social entrepreneurs from Brooklyn. Artists from Williamsburg. Musicians and teachers from Queens. Executives, editors, professors, models, investors, and journalists from Manhattan. And, around 10 p.m. or so, even the Brooklyn-raised rapper Busta Rhymes showed up uninvited, albeit keeping very low-key. The vibe was familial and human: artistic expression and a safe space for being human crowded-out all egos. Sketchiness or douchery would have prompted ejection. Art was the Trojan Horse and created the human space to connect in genuine ways, apart from the titles, colors, class, and social status.

By the time Questlove spun his last few songs, the dance floor was hopping and the room filled with warmth. An entrepreneur from San Francisco leaned back in her silver dress holding a glass of wine with a big smile, radiating. People also gathered around the sides of the room at small tables or in conversation. The fire dancer from Harlem, traveling that night without her torches, talked with a hedge-fund investor from

Chicago. It was already one of those nights full of magic, when everyone seemed to be smiling or laughing.

There was something to celebrate too: the birth of a cultural insurgency.

Amid the sea of people surrounding the stage area, one head poked out above the crowd. It was the unmistakable large and well-coiffed noggin of Henry Timms. Back then, Henry was a mid-manager of sorts at the 92nd Street Y, the New York cultural center. He looked and acted British in pretty much every way: from the emotional reserve to the pasty yet energetic face to the slightly lumpy body (which he would later transform into a svelte runner's frame) to a nearly incomparably brilliant mind and wit. Look: he was British, all right. But Henry was quick to note that he was also a descendant of Francis Scott Key, and had a real patriotism about his adopted home.

Earlier that year, Henry had a big idea: after Thanksgiving, Black Friday, and Cyber Monday, why not have a day of giving, give it a hashtag, and call it #GivingTuesday?

The idea seemed intuitive and timely, a constructive response to a culture of greed and consumerism. So I joined the founding team. Black Sheep, or BLK SHP as our vowelless logo now read, was in. We believed that people had significant reservoirs of generosity and, more importantly, an unquenched desire to be a part of something larger than themselves. In a cultural moment that neared "peak individualism," we aspired to be part of a movement that would help shift culture from "I" to "we."

Now, some people change the world because they allow themselves to think so big that it's just at the edge of impossible. Create an international day of giving? Who thinks up shit like that? That would be this bloke Henry Timms, mid-manager at a nonprofit on the Upper East Side of New York. Henry turned out to be a visionary leader who thought as big as the American entrepreneurial spirit, with the class, sophistication, and cool English accent to comfort cautious skeptics. We didn't fully realize it at the time, but Henry was another black sheep in wolf's clothes.

It wasn't long before we called our little core crew working on the Giving Tuesday team a "motley posse." We also had nicknames. As we went around the horn on calls, Henry would lightly prod us to do the things that only each of us could do to get shit done (GSD). Aaron Hirsch (aka The Smoker) built the social media strategy. Sharon Feder (The COO) functioned like our chief operating officer. Aaron Sherinian (Tuxedo) led our public relations and communications. Meanwhile, Henry's right hand at the 92Y, Asha Curran (The Dancer), acted as project manager and danced across worlds to make sure the visions could become reality. To all of our great joy, Henry led with his brilliant wit, as well as an uncanny ability to get each of us misfits to play our best role at just the right time. It was a bit like we were a rock band that needed to become an orchestra. Henry was our "Conductor."

The basic path to success was to get as many people and organizations as possible to use the hashtag "#GivingTuesday" on social media on November 27, 2012 to encourage generosity to social causes. We focused on mostly small gifts: $5 or $10. Meanwhile, partners like the Gates Foundation or LinkedIn could provide matching funds. So in order to achieve credibility and scale, we needed partners. Lots of partners. The UN Foundation and 92Y were just the start. We needed credibility for the idea from places like the Gates Foundation. We had a good story

to tell. In just a few months, we pulled together about 750 partners in 46 states, mostly nonprofits who wanted to raise more
money online.

That first year felt a bit like we were on a kamikaze mission:
either the idea was going to take, or it would crash and burn.
But we never thought about failure. We were having a blast,
with the nicknames and the "motley posse" and all, and the
idea surely had legs, even if establishing a global day of giving
was extremely ambitious.

We were doing it for all the Uncle Joes out there who were
tired of the culture of greed and who wanted to *do something*
about it—to have some agency, and not feel helpless, hopeless,
or victimized—to be a part of the solution, rather than the problem. We were doing it for all the social innovators in places like
Detroit, ravished by globalization, who were rebuilding their cities one block and one building at a time.

Just a few months earlier, five of us Black Sheep jour-
neyed into the bowels of the city and stood outside a giant,
2,200,000-square-foot, seven-building industrial complex, shiv-
ering. The building was so rusted and shattered from the outside
that it seemed impossible that life was inside. I'm not sure what
I expected, but the reality was a lot worse than expected. The
Russell Industrial Center was built in 1925, we were told, and
was used by the Dodge brothers to make auto bodies. Later Ford;
then Packard Motors. I've only seen pictures of Dresden after
World War II, but that's how most of Detroit felt: bombed out,
hollowed out, a shell of its former self, decrepit . . . dead.

And yet . . .

Detroit still had Eminem and grit, and was still the shit. For
a city that suffered its worst crucible during the 1980s crack

epidemic, there had been pretty much only one way to go: up. After a conversion, The Russell Industrial Center had a million square feet of studio space and lofts for artists, entrepreneurs, social innovators, artisans, and craftsmen—the social bacteria drawn to Detroit's cheap rents and grit. Inside, the Russell was dark and musty, made even darker by the dark green walls, as our voices echoed through the hallways that seemed to stretch a quarter of a mile or more. It felt like the setting of one of those low-budget paranormal movies.

Coming upon the first open doorway on our right, we entered cautiously. It felt like an abandoned bunker, full of dust and dirt on the floor, with only scattered business cards and old bills to indicate that life had been there before, and in what form. Noticing telephone bills sent to the attention of a business address, we figured the previous tenant must have been an entrepreneur or social entrepreneur. They had probably been gone for six months, at least, by the time we descended—perhaps out of the dingy industrial space and into a proper office.

That's when it hit me. This was the womb of American renewal. We were in the womb of American renewal.

If Detroit were personified in the 1980s and 1990s, it might resemble a homeless drug addict without an education. Imagine a city with nearly 100,000 vacant buildings, over 30,000 empty houses, and something like 90,000 vacant lots. Pummeled by job losses from globalization in the 1980s, about half the city's Black men were unemployed before the crack epidemic arrived in 1984 and ravaged the city. The depths of hopelessness and despair that followed were nearly unprecedented in recent US history.

And yet . . .

Detroit became a beacon for a group of creative moths, drawn to the cheap rents, the collaborative and supportive entrepreneurial community, and the city's never-say-die spirit. They got studios or temporary office space in places like the Russell Industrial Center, where they worked on creating everything from sculptures to furniture to nonprofits to small businesses. While those LBO dorks worked on spreadsheets in New York, Greenwich, and London, Detroit became ground zero for reinventing America from the ground up.

We bled for these grassroots innovators. Giving Tuesday was all about supporting them and so many others all over the country and the world who are forging a more generous and compassionate culture.

One of the coolest things about moving into "get shit done" mode with Giving Tuesday was seeing the loose tribe of Black Sheep spring into action. It was like prying open the cap of lightning in a bottle. Beth Comstock helped get GE involved. We didn't care if it was Ponyride, a creative incubator for social innovators in Detroit, or a Rotary Club in Kansas City; we were passionate about mobilizing local partners. All through this tribe of Black Sheep. Whether it was his Francis Scott Key heritage or something else, the Conductor seemed to bleed for grassroots America as much as we did. And, in perhaps our biggest coup, we worked with black sheep inside the White House to secure a Presidential endorsement—an important credibility stamp.

The whole Giving Tuesday experience showed us that a relatively carefree, crazy, motley posse of Black Sheep misfits, incapable of doing all that much on their own, had the potential to ignite a movement.

And it worked. It really worked. That first year, #GivingTuesday raised $10 million from hundreds of partners. The White House even endorsed the idea, albeit only reluctantly following a significant pressure campaign from some Black Sheep. The next year, we tapped a few Black Sheep in Europe to take the generosity movement to that continent, where it spread like wildfire. Even that was just the beginning.

The true timeliness of the idea turned out to be that, back then, nonprofits had very little idea of what they were doing when it came to using social media or raising money online. We provided nonprofits with a toolkit to set up online donations and, more importantly, an annual day of online giving with its own hashtag—#GivingTuesday—that gave nonprofits an excuse to shamelessly ask people for money on that day.

Now, if you were to have told me then that ten years later Giving Tuesday would be a global movement in over 100 countries that has raised over $10 billion for social good causes, only a small part of me would have believed it. That vision and values never wavered: to be part of a global generosity movement that would help shift culture from "I" to "we." The renaissance and cultural awakening we dreamed about formed its foundational elements. We knew that the people had significant reservoirs of generosity and, sure enough, people were talking about it everywhere—from Mobile to Pittsburgh to Detroit.

Henry came to see Black Sheep as an A-Team for social good, and he nicknamed me Hannibal. I had to Google the reference, but Hannibal was the cigar-smoking ringleader of the A-Team, the 1980s TV show about a unit of four former special forces soldiers. The A-Team had been court-martialed for "a crime they did not commit," then escaped prison and became mercenary vigilantes. Hannibal was known for saying, "I love it when a plan comes together," a line I found great joy in using whenever possible. Henry's A-Team analogy was perfect: we were such a bunch of castaways, incapable of doing much of anything alone, yet together could take on the world.

After the music performances in Liberty Hall that night, we bestowed Henry with a proper conductor's jacket: a long, black leather coat with gold leafing on the collar. I don't think I ever saw Henry have as good a time as he did that night.

My room at the Ace Hotel happened to be one of the largest rooms in the hotel, so the afterparty flowed there. The fire dancer. The hedge-fund investor. A bunch of artists. The rest of our team. Maybe a dozen people streamed into my room, just being human. Our own "Churchill," Matthew Bishop, a portly British writer and editor at *The Economist* who played a key role as a media influencer during the launch of Giving Tuesday, sat in a chair, holding a whiskey and pontificating. Meanwhile, the hedge-fund investor and I stood talking on the other side of the room, not far from the fire dancer, who was talking with a few others.

No one hooked up. It was just clean, human, creative fun.

The Black Sheep had arrived.

CHAPTER NINE

INTO THE ABYSS

W e were plotting the next phase of Black Sheep when something happened that shaped all that followed, and was also an extremely humbling reminder of what almost all our families face inside the matrix. I was visiting my dad at my family's mountain house in Dutch Flat, a tiny town not far from Lake Tahoe, founded in 1851 by mostly German immigrants during the California Gold Rush era. The house where I grew up is about twenty-five minutes away, and Uncle Joe and Aunt Liz live about ten minutes away. At its peak, Dutch Flat had about 100,000 people living in the area, many prospecting for gold. After the Gold Rush, everyone left and the town never really changed much after that. Today, it has a year-round population of about 160 people. There's a cluster of old buildings in town, including an unused Masonic Hall and Odd Fellows Hall, and a store called the Trading Post, which stands beside a cubby-hole-sized US post office. Across the street from the Trading Post is the old Dutch Flat Hotel, built in 1852 and striking in its red-and-white paint.

When I arrived, quite frayed from exhaustion, both Dad and Linda, his wife of later years, frowned and the mood felt heavy. Finally, it was said, we could have a proper visit. Perhaps it would be our last. As I tried to rest a bit, lying on a couch in the small house, I heard Dad talking on the phone in the other room with an old friend. What I caught of their conversation made me think: it sounds like it might be their last.

Dad had cancer.

It was skin cancer and although it was still at a relatively early stage, Dad thought he was going to die. He had a tendency to be overly-dramatic, so there was room for optimism, but for weeks I hadn't really slept. I had been on a plane for months on a book tour, crisscrossing the globe, and my fragile exhaustion was obvious. Mom was more than a bit worried. Mothers seem to know when something is about to go very wrong, but unfortunately Mom wasn't around this time, my parents having divorced about fifteen years prior.

It was 2014, more than ten years since I had left London, Summit Partners, and the predictable path. It was a stage of life when I had come to understand many of the underlying factors that once motivated that suit-wearing, eager beaver; that insecure overachiever. In this new chapter, I aspired to live my values and the highest version of myself, and no longer gave a shit about the awards, accolades, and achievements that I once did, and that Dad still treasured. But there was still another big trauma in my family lineage, which had been beneath the surface, mostly hidden in shadows until that day.

After lunch, the three of us decided to take a walk around town. It was a warm day, inviting a sweat after only a few minutes of walking. By the time we made it to my grandma's old house on the other side of town, I was already feeling a bit lightheaded. That's when what felt like an important thought came to me.

We walked past the community center and church on Main Street, then took a right up another street that would soon pass the old house my grandmother used to own. Named Wild Honey, it was a cute two-story white house with green trim and a corrugated aluminum roof that was used mostly as a summer house. This is where my father spent some of the happiest days of his life, as a boy. He spent his days running around the spacious lawn in the back or scurrying up to the community pool, often barefoot, a quarter-mile away.

That's when the notion struck me: it was here, in this quaint, soulful town, surrounded by pine trees, where Dad seemed to have felt most free and alive as a boy, and most at peace as an older man. I was suddenly overcome by emotion.

"Dad, I think you need to forgive Grandma." I blurted it out, unsure of exactly where the words came from, but they felt profoundly true.

I had barely known Grandma Dale. She died when I was ten years old. But what I did know was that Dad really had his differences with her for reasons that would take years for me to understand. I had never met anyone who seemed to despise their mother like Dad despised Grandma Dale. Yet as I thought about how we were perhaps on one of his last laps through the town he loved most, something deep inside me welled up and I begged for him to forgive his mother. I didn't want him to die with that burden on his soul.

"Forgive her, Dad," I begged, and started to cry. That too was really odd since I rarely cry. "Forgive her!"

I knew that Dad resented Grandma's alcoholism, yet that was just the start since the brunt of her addiction hit after he left for college. Dad seemed to especially resent how her desire for social status and recognition had basically bankrupted the family, especially as she and his father had aged. In her quest for her own public recognition, she had put a lot of pressure on my dad, even suggesting that he might one day be President of the United States. Imagining my father as an innocent boy with so much pressure on him brought tears to my eyes. It also helped explain why he had put so much pressure on me especially, his oldest of two sons, to achieve.

Something else hid in the shadows of our family history; something that we almost never talked about. My grandmother's sister had something in her closet, as did my father: a history of mental health episodes. It too was part of our shared lineage. The only thing I can remember about my father's mental health breakdown in his early 40s was that he took my brother and me, then young boys, to our closest family friend's house to spend the night. I couldn't understand what was happening. Years later, I learned that Dad had gone through some sort of mental health episode, exhibiting a paranoia-like concern that the state police were going to find traces of marijuana inside a decorative Indian headdress in his judicial office in Sacramento. It seems Dad was convinced that if this happened, it would end his quest to be on the California State Supreme Court, his lifetime career goal. Although he got treatment, I never knew the full extent of what had happened, either the crisis or its resolution, because he never wanted to talk about it. The stigma and shame were too great.

That day outside of Grandma Dale's Wild Honey home, as I cried and cried, it was apparently my turn.

Dad didn't know what to do with my outburst. He wanted to keep walking, as did Linda. But I refused, or couldn't, and so we stood on the road beside Grandma's old house, the 75- or 80-degree day radiating up from the paved road. I cried, feeling hysterical, until I collapsed on the street. It occurred to me that I might die there, almost as if I was underwater and drowning and might run out of air. This all lasted maybe two or three minutes, until I realized that after my outburst of emotion I was still breathing. Lying in the street. Alive.

Now what?

The next part is a bit hazy.

After standing up and making sure my limbs and head were still intact, I was still crying and felt delirious. Through some combination of exhaustion and emotion, I experienced a dream-like state. After weeks of sleep deprivation, I felt almost outside of my body. My mind whirred with images: about my dad and grandmother, about Linda, and even about the driver of a car that passed by who looked like Cousin Nick. I could register that Dad and Linda were very concerned. Linda tried to calm me down while Dad went back to the house to get the car.

As I looked into Linda's compassionate blue eyes, I saw an empathy I had not fully seen before. My parents were married for nearly thirty years before Dad decided he wanted a new life. He and Linda found one: a life of constant travels, adventures, and hedonism; two aging Baby Boomers making up for lost time, still running from their pain. Yet the longer I stared into Linda's eyes, another intuition welled up: that she wasn't trustworthy. I was certain of it. And I ran over to the bushes next to the house to hide.

Needless to say, Linda was pretty confused.

The crying subsided. I felt the depths of my exhaustion and found a shady patch of grass to sit on. By the time Dad returned with the car, I was calm as a cucumber. And as we drove to the hospital, I just stared out the window, listless. It was an odd juxtaposition: just a half hour after being hysterical, I felt complete emotional peace.

The doctors in the emergency room ran a bunch of tests and concluded that I was fatigued and perhaps slightly traumatized by Dad's cancer and failing health. In that antiseptic environment of white walls, doctors in blue smocks, and white fluorescent lighting, my mind was navigating two alternate realities: one in which I was very calm and grounded; another in which my active imagination was demanding attention. It was just Dad and me in the exam room for a while, and I told him, in one breath, that he was one of my heroes, and in the next asked him why he was still with Linda. I confided that there was a part of me that worried she was trying to control him.

The doctor prescribed sleep medication, and we got back to the house by early evening. After a light dinner, it was time for bed, and Linda gave me a sleeping pill, as prescribed by the doctor. It was a warm night, a hot night even, so I stripped down to my boxers and lay atop the sheets of the bed.

Man, it was hot. Uncomfortably hot. So I decided to move to the room downstairs, which was ten, fifteen degrees cooler. But before I could do so, Linda, who by then was understandably exhausted and raw, gave me another sleeping pill.

It was, I know now, a well-intended gesture. There was a sense that if only we could all get some sleep, everything would be better in the morning. That said, I was supposed to have only one pill. And that's about when things started to get even more interesting.

The downstairs guest room had its own little bathroom and was a prized spot during the warm summer nights. The room also had a closet, and in that closet was Dad's gun safe.

Dad had loved guns since he was a boy watching Will Rogers and western movies. He paid for part of law school by selling a few guns, he told us, and then acquired more. It was one of Dad's impulsive buying habits that drove Linda batty. She hated guns. I agreed with her. In my beyond-exhausted, over-medicated, and overly-sensitized state while lying in that bed, I came to a conviction: that Dad might hurt himself with his guns. My brother, Linda, and I had all had that opinion at one point or another. So I got out of bed, still in my boxers, and grabbed the keys to the safe and hid them.

At roughly the same time, it occurred to Linda, who for many obvious reasons had become a basket case, that I was in the room with the gun safe, and she panicked. So Dad came down, knocked on the door, and asked me to sleep upstairs. *Ugh!* What a pain in the ass! I was just settling in downstairs and now I had to move back up into the heat.

I experienced Linda as mostly pure nervous energy. So when, as I moved back upstairs, she gave me *yet another* sleeping pill, I swallowed it. I was so over this long day. So after popping the keys to the gun cabinet into the top drawer of the dresser, I hopped into bed and started to trail off to sleep.

If only.

I was just about asleep when Dad knocked on the door and asked me where I put the keys to the gun cabinet. I told him I didn't want him to hurt himself. He persisted and I gave him the keys, but not before Linda dialed 9-1-1.

Ohhh, shit! We were going back into *The Twilight Zone* for the second time that day.

I could hear Linda on the phone in the other room, so I went into the hallway and picked up the extra phone. I listened in just as she was telling the 9-1-1 operator that I had the keys to the gun cabinet. She was saying she felt threatened, or something along those lines. I calmly tried to interject that no such thing was going on, but by then Linda had blown a gasket. It was as if we had both completely maxed out emotionally, simultaneously. But in that moment and in my frame of mind, I decided to do what I was certain any self-respecting American would do: I pulled the phone cord out of the wall.

After all that, everything felt surprisingly calm. I felt calm. The house felt calm. The night felt calm. As Dad and Linda gathered in their room, I decided to make some herbal tea. The police would arrive soon, I figured. As the water warmed on the stove, I stood in front of the open windows of the dining room, which faced out on the nearly pitch-black driveway that wound through some trees onto the county road about fifty yards beyond. It was a dark, moonless night and the water hadn't even boiled before I could hear footsteps coming up the driveway, and around the house from both sides.

"I love you," I chanted, *"I lovvvveee you!"* This felt courageous for being true.

Shit was definitely starting to feel very real as the officer, in efficient, even mechanical moves, pushed my head into the back of her patrol car. I had just been escorted down the driveway in handcuffs, accompanied by two sheriff's officers and the half-dozen members of the town's volunteer fire department. As I sat in silence, with only my thoughts, I wasn't sure if or when I would see my family again. I knew I was over-medicated on a sleep aid, although I didn't realize just how heavily. I wondered if it was all a plot to institutionalize me.

It had been a day of firsts, and it wasn't over yet.

It was the first time I had ever been arrested. That was something of a milestone. After all, I was known as one of the local kids who had "made it." What's more, my dad had been a judge, as had been his father, whom we called Grandpa Judge. Growing up, I had dutifully avoided potential arrests. Now, I was 38 years old: old enough to be considered highly accomplished, yet young enough to be discovering parts of my humanity.

As we turned and walked down the driveway together as a group, I knew I would never forget this "perp walk." Despite my bone-deep fatigue and the day's unimaginable turn of events, the moment was somehow completely novel and memorable. As we reached the end of the driveway, leading onto a county road, one sheriff's car was a K-9 unit, and a dog was in the back seat. It was barking hysterically.

Everything went quiet for a minute or so, sitting alone in the back of that patrol car—except for the dog continuing to bark like crazy in the other car. The dog seemed to get it.

Clearly the plot to institutionalize me, if it did exist, was well on track by that point. I was in the back seat of the sheriff's car and we were headed to some hospital. I didn't know where. What

I did know was that the handcuffs really hurt. I tried to wrestle my arms free. With that, the officer immediately pulled over off the interstate at the next off-ramp and called an ambulance. Once transferred to the ambulance, I felt relieved to no longer be with such an alien-like creature who seemed so inhuman.

That I was on a path to learn certain realities about my mental health that had eluded me for a lifetime didn't change the fact that being handcuffed by officers who seemed animated strictly by muscle memory was deeply unsettling.

Mental health is one of those things that affects everyone, certainly every family, yet almost no one feels comfortable talking openly about it. The stigmas can be deep, intergenerational, and enveloped by shame. Only the lucky few end up getting proper treatment, while many end up in the back of police cars or in hospitals, dealing with emotionless people taking reports.

While transferring from police cruiser to ambulance, I was entering an abyss from which some never emerge.

My first ride in an ambulance would probably have been more fun if I wasn't handcuffed to the gurney. I mean, the EMTs seemed nice enough, given the circumstances. They had spread me out as on a cross, handcuffing me to the sides of the gurney and bracing my legs. And *man* those handcuffs hurt. It felt like my wrists were bleeding, and I pleaded with the EMT sitting in the back with me to help. Unlike the cold sheriff officer, his eyes and kind words conveyed empathy. But regulations and protocols being regulations and protocols, he just couldn't. The only thing that came to mind was to ask him, "Are you guys actors?"

He was trying to be supportive, shifting my body and holding my wrists as we careened down the interstate. I figured that

I was being taken to a mental hospital, or institute, or something. That would be a first too. It all felt like a dark side of the matrix, another side of "the system" I hadn't really seen before: the inhuman cops, the intense pain of handcuffs digging into my bones, the ambulance, the uncertain destination.

It was all interesting, I kept thinking—the whole thing. This is what happened when, like so many before me, you stepped into this other side of the system. People in need of empathic care routinely get thrown in the back of cop cars, handcuffed to gurneys, treated like shit, and then grilled by mental health workers completely devoid of compassion.

I am getting a bit ahead of myself, ahead of a few other firsts. But by the time I was spread-eagle on that gurney, I was coming to understand America's mental health system in a whole new way— even coming to understand the country I love in a whole new way. If in one part of the matrix I had been for years among those Americans who had "made it," there had existed alongside it a byzantine set of inhuman systems, seemingly devoid of empathy.

Which was the dream, and which was the real America? What I didn't understand, not then, not right away, was that I was just discovering my full humanity.

⚡

When my eyes slowly opened two days later, I couldn't even tell if it was morning. My whole body ached to its core, as if I had the worst flu, such that it was hard to sit up. Judging by the noise, there seemed to be plenty of activity in the hallway, and I fumbled around for my glasses. Everything seemed blurry around the edges and everything hurt—like, really hurt. My mind no longer wondered about "the system." My imagination seemed gone, surrendering to the requirements of survival, including my genuine hunger after not having eaten much of anything in 48 hours, the only calories or liquids having come by way of whatever they had pumped through an IV into my arm that first night.

The good news was that the daytime staff seemed friendly and kind, especially compared to the memories of the robotic terror of an officer, as well as the mental health workers. I knew I had been injected with a strong cocktail of drugs the night before, and only later learned that it rivaled a kind of tranquilizer often given to horses. I emerged from my room and after a meal, I did what the other patients were doing: I walked the hallway that followed the perimeter of the floor, taking laps.

The other patients tended to pair off or cluster in small groups, and either walk together, talk, or watch TV. There were two TV lounges, one at each end of the floor. It wasn't quite like what I might have expected had someone asked me a month prior what happened in a psychiatric hospital. Maybe it was just the floor I was on, but no one seemed schizophrenic or anything like that. Mostly, the people I met, all of us in our blue smocks, seemed sensitive and creative. As nightfall approached, I was actually starting to have a good time, and was fascinated by the whole experience, which I told Mom and my girlfriend when I was allowed a couple of phone calls. Surely there were a lot of black sheep in the mental ward!

I shuffled around and around, lap by lap, until dusk brought back some painful memories from the previous nights. This night was different, though. I had made a couple new friends, including a guy roughly my age who seemed smart and plenty functional, as well as a woman wearing purplish glasses who was extremely gentle and kind. They had been there longer and educated me. No longer was I alone in this alternate reality.

Something else was happening that night. Something profound. Something historic that drew everyone to the TV lounges. CNN had descended on Ferguson, a suburb outside St. Louis, Missouri. We learned that a Ferguson police officer had shot and killed Michael Brown, a Black man, triggering significant social upheaval. From the images we were seeing, Ferguson looked like a war zone. National Guard armored vehicles drove through a town ablaze while heavily-armed soldiers patrolled the streets. The sensitive woman in the purplish glasses could hardly watch.

Something about it all felt seminal. I mean, what was this little suburban town burning in the middle of nowhere America? It wasn't Detroit or Los Angeles this time; Ferguson was a cultural and racial fault line smack-dab in the middle of America. And it was all we could talk about, all these sensitive people walking around in blue smocks. They squirmed seeing Ferguson go up in flames. They cringed at the sight of troops and tanks driving through the streets. They felt for humanity at that moment, as if there had been a massive disruption in our collective wellbeing.

We quiet, blue smock-wearing patients were watching in the quiet of our floor as soldiers armed to the hilt with weapons and armor patrolled Ferguson. And we were the crazy ones?

Suddenly, it seemed like the whole experience of the last few days had happened for a reason. Perhaps it was so I could see what life was like on another side of the matrix, places I never expected to go, and encounter people I never expected to meet. Perhaps it was to see the inhumanity that can character-ize America's police and mental health system. Perhaps it was to see the black sheep that society so often pushes out of sight and locks away. Perhaps it was to internalize something of what was happening in Ferguson, Missouri that night, a vast system that divides and separates us rather than a creed that seeks common humanity. And there was Ferguson, at the epicenter of a fault line of one of America's great cultural chasms: race.

I figured it had all happened to teach me something—or many things. My family lineage needed healing, and so did America's; both required humility and vulnerability.

Seeing the doctor again the next day, the psychiatrist on the floor gave me his diagnosis. He said I exhibited "manic ten-dencies," which was a symptom of bipolar. A manic episode, he explained, looked like what I had experienced outside Grandma Dale's house. Often correlated with sleep deprivation, it is when your mood swings to a dramatically elevated state—typically with spikes in energy, creativity, and self-confidence. Reflecting on my past few years, the idea of manic tendencies mostly made sense, although I hadn't experienced the depressive swings that characterized most bipolar diagnoses. That aside, I just thanked him, and he prescribed lithium as a mood stabilizer. I was grate-ful to be treated. I had been inside the system looking out; now, I was just a person in blue smocks walking into the world again, feeling strangely enlightened and energized by the experience.

I had never felt so human.

There, standing on the busy streets of San Francisco in my blue smocks, my most vulnerable state, I accepted it all fully. I accepted all the things about the past few days and my diagnosis and that the white-sheep world too often stigmatizes and judges harshly. In my most vulnerable state, I felt renewed conviction to expose the systems that stifle and dehumanize us all.

I wasn't going to starve; everything else would be gravy.

Thankfully, I got treatment. America, meanwhile, had a mental health crisis; a spiritual crisis, deep within its core. I wanted to go to Ferguson and back to Detroit. What gave me faith that we could make a difference was the power of humanity: the often unheard and unseen yet incredible people who wanted to do things differently. The black sheep who wanted to heal themselves and break the generational curses so they could pass their children a new lineage.

Maybe that's you.

CHAPTER TEN

CONNECTING THE DISCONNECTED

W e pulled into Ferguson, Missouri at about 9 a.m. on Mother's Day, 2015. It was a warm day; a bit humid, even. The town looked surprisingly beautiful.

Nine months had passed since the upheaval of the previous summer. Compared to the images of the protests that we had seen on TV the summer before, Ferguson, about twelve miles north of downtown St. Louis looked a lot like attractive American suburbs everywhere: nice homes with neat lawns of natural grass, and parks with playgrounds and greenery. With a population of about 21,000 people, nearly 70% of the residents were Black, while most of the remaining 30% were White.

We had no idea what the hell we were doing. What we did know was we were a band of misfits, frustrated artists-entrepreneurs, questing for new ways of doing things, even just being, that the system wasn't listening to. We were in search of America's "true north," which we understood as seeking new stories and ways of re-imagining America from the bottom up.

Ferguson was the fourteenth city we visited on a seventeen-city tour that began in Austin, Texas, before circling the South and Southeastern seaboard, before trekking through the Midwest into the center of the country. We felt like we were on a mission from God, somewhere between *The Blues Brothers* and *Travels with Charley*. "We're getting the band back together!" we joked, echoing Dan Aykroyd and John Belushi. We always had generous amounts of fun, even if our mission was big. You see, we were artists, and we knew America was experiencing a midlife crisis of sorts. There we were, a motley posse of misfits, gliding through the Midwest on a rock star's vintage tour bus. We weren't dispensing answers. As storytellers, we listened and observed. We were connecting. Mostly, we were doing something to confront that feeling we encountered everywhere: what got you here won't get you there.

Despite the peaceful day, there were remnants of the protests, rioting, and upheaval from the previous summer. Some of the downtown buildings were still boarded up with plywood, now covered by graffiti. One spray-painted plywood board read: "Injustice anywhere is a threat to justice everywhere," the words surrounded by red flowers. Another read: "Hakuna matata," the Swahili phrase for no worries or troubles. And next to this phrase: "Peace begins with a smile," alongside an American flag.

To put you in the spirit of the quest we were on, imagine an old rocker's tour bus careening through miles and miles of farms and urban jungles across America, as *Listen to the Music* by The Doobie Brothers plays. At any given time about ten

Black Sheep all on creative life paths rotated in and out of the bus—a mix of artists, entrepreneurs, storytellers, and the hopeful. What we had in common was the mission, the quest, the belief that doing something, anything, was an important start. And we had the bus.

We were supposed to have been on one of Willie Nelson & Family's old tour buses called Me and Paul, a custom-built 1983 Silver Eagle once used by Willie's drummer Paul English with an On the Road Again destination sign and an iconic eagle painted on the back. But dammit if that bus wasn't still in the shop when we pushed off from Austin.

So we ended up on Barbara Mandrell's old bus, used by the famous country music singer who was popular in the 1970s-80s. The bus looked normal from the outside, with intermittent brown and white paint all around, above the silver siding of the under-carriage.

All bets were off on the inside. Ostrich leather walls, little ceiling lights everywhere, and a decadent bathroom with a silver sink and reflective steel siding. The bedroom in the back of the bus took the cake: a queen-sized bed surrounded by mirrors. We eventually nicknamed her The Glitter Bus.

Well, the arrival of a bunch of Black Sheep on a Glitter Bus was local news just about everywhere we went. In Austin, Texas, Matthew Dowd from *ABC News*, wearing a Bob Dylan t-shirt, joined dozens of social innovators and artists to send us off. In Mobile, Alabama, Mayor Sandy Stimpson stood on top of a state trooper's car, taking photos of the Glitter Bus as we entered his city, and then he showed us around himself. In Greenville, South Carolina, hundreds of people came out for a full day of festivities around the arrival of the Black Sheep, complete with live music. Television commentators would announce, "The Black Sheep are coming to town!"

It was all a bit wild, and to us it felt like a movement in the making. And then there were hours of downtime.

In the back cabin of the bus, I would stare out the window at the countryside streaming by, and ponder the future of America. The country was just so damn complex, almost as diverse as humanity itself. America's spirit of Manifest Destiny and commercial progress had created the richest country on Earth, yet by the twenty-first century the country was obviously extremely disconnected and lacked a spiritual grounding.

Our focus, our fascination, our yearning was to find the people who were reinventing themselves and their communities—and America—from the ground up.

As Harold O'Neal and I walked around Ferguson that glorious Mother's Day morning with the filmmaker Patrick Bresnan, we gravitated toward Wellspring Church on South Florissant Road. O'Neal, who grew up in public housing in Kansas City as the son and nephew of Black Panther leaders, had become an accomplished jazz pianist and composer. O'Neal's musical gifts were just the beginning of his many talents, as he often liked to remind (and show) people. He was a black belt in karate, a nearly professional break-dancer, and could usually solve a Rubik's Cube in a minute or two. A born performer, Harold O'Neal loved connecting with people on tour.

"We are trying to make our mothers *very* happy today," the greeter out front of Wellspring Church said, wearing a purple t-shirt that said "I AM WELL" in white letters. "We're serving 'em assorted donuts, juice, and coffee and milk, and the men are in action!"

Right then, a tan Ford Taurus pulled up and out stepped an older woman dressed in a lovely white dress and black hat, black shoes, and a black and white polka-dot scarf. She was a vision of splendor.

"Well, alright!" the greeter enthused, stepping toward the street, "Do I need to come out there 'cause I don't want you to trip?'"

She let out a big cackle. "Not in the white today!" she replied. Laughing, she made her way over to him, hugging and kissing him. "Good morning, my brother!" she exclaimed.

She was a real light.

"Good morning, saints!" she said as she took a few more steps toward the fellowship hall behind the church, then found herself in an embrace with another greeter. He moved to let go; she held tight.

"I'm sorry; I didn't give you the blessings that you deserve," she said as she held onto him. "Ohhh! Blessings to you, my brother. My brother from another mother!"

Everyone laughed.

As it turned out, there were a lot of activities happening at Wellspring Church that morning. In one part, the Sunday service kicked off, with sounds of sermon, song, and prayer. In the other part of the church a large group of young people gathered. In the adjacent fellowship hall, the kids signed Mother's Day cards, worked on art projects, and attended Sunday School classes.

Back outside the church, sharing with those who asked that we were Black Sheep, and explaining what the hell that meant, something happened that happened often on the tour.

"I'm a Black Sheep!" a young man proclaimed as he raised his hand to shield his eyes from the sun. He was seated on a curb next to the main walkway next to the church and couldn't help but overhear our conversation. He was also wearing a purple "I AM WELL" t-shirt.

At each stop on tour, countless people told us they had been black sheep all their lives, yet had always felt alone. Or they would ask, "Where have you been all my life?"

That moment outside the church, though, was a little different. Danny McGinnist Jr. was a fairly typical 19-year-old in many ways, and he acted like it. He was an adolescent seemingly addicted to staring into his phone, mostly absorbed with his world. It didn't take long before he was talking up a storm, though. As we discussed being a black sheep and about his own artistry, however, his mood bordered on hopelessness. He opened his wallet to show us that it was empty—an aspiring artist who couldn't afford supplies; only a sketchbook.

That was just the beginning. Danny told us he had been homeless off and on for some years. He seemed to like talking, and that we listened. He was visiting Wellspring that day with his godparents, who lived in Ferguson, and Danny had volunteered to help teach one of the art classes. But, he added quickly, he wasn't a fine artist—not yet at least. He mostly dabbled in producing music.

We asked him if he had witnessed the upheaval in Ferguson last year, and he had indeed seen a lot of it. That's when Danny became our teacher.

"Can you believe they sent tanks into town?" he asked plaintively.

That prospect I had never fully considered, especially not in America. Just trying to imagine tanks rolling into my small rural hometown defied imagination. I remembered seeing images of the tanks in Ferguson the year before, as we stood around the TV watching CNN in our blue smocks in the mental ward. There was something shocking about seeing tanks. As shocking as it was to see the looting or rioting, was there any greater symbol of America's violent and militaristic underbelly than the felt need to dispatch tanks on fellow citizens? The inhumanity of America's mental health system paled in comparison.

Danny was now gesturing and speaking with passion as he educated us about the protests. As the sun and humidity announced midday, beads of sweat appeared on his brow. "Why would we ever destroy the Little Caesars?" he asked with a quizzical look, then enthused, "We *love* Little Caesars! Those were *outsiders* who came into town!"

Danny had been homeless off-and-on since he was twelve. He lived in his car for long periods or stayed in the basement of his sister's house or with his godparents, who were attending Wellspring for the service. That's how Danny ended up outside church that day. Yet much as he loved his godparents, organized religion wasn't Danny's thing.

Art was.

As a boy, he drew relentlessly, filling dozens of sketchbooks. He *had to* create, sketching thousands of people, including countless nudes. Sometimes he found a way to pay models, while others agreed to pose for free. He could not stop sketching. It was primal. One day, one of Danny's high school teachers asked him if he had heard of Jean-Michel Basquiat. The parallels between the two artists were interesting, if not obvious. Basquiat had also been homeless during his younger days as a graffiti-artist in New York City, before he became one of the most famous American painters of the 1980s, and one of the world's most celebrated Black painters.

That teacher was how Basquiat became an important role model to Danny, and Danny would eventually honor him with a tattoo of the artist's famous "T-Rex" on his right arm.

The more Danny shared his story, the more I felt like he was a kindred spirit. Danny was definitely a black sheep. Hell, he could have just jumped on the bus with us when we left for Kansas City, our next stop, and fit right into our little crew. What none of us, including Danny, had any idea of was that he was something of a prodigy. He didn't even start painting until later that year. On that bright, beautiful Mother's Day, however, it didn't matter. What we knew was that we already felt connected by the spirit of the path less-traveled.

As Danny described some of the scenes and his feelings from the previous August, it was impossible to not feel his pain and anguish from seeing his community torn apart. Everything had come to a roiling head when a White police officer shot and killed Michael Brown, an unarmed Black eighteen-year-old. Danny didn't have any money, but he did give a damn about his community, as evidenced by his showing up to teach kids art that morning.

Just being there helped me understand why this tiny suburb smack in the middle of America had gone up in flames. Even walking into the McDonald's on West Florissant Avenue, about a quarter-mile from the Target parking lot that the National Guard used as a staging area, you could cut the tension with a knife. No one seemed relaxed. Michael Brown was suspected to take part in a robbery next door at the Ferguson Market & Liquor shortly before he was shot and killed by Officer Darren Wilson a short drive away.

Inside that McDonald's, it was the complete opposite vibe from Wellspring Church, which felt so safe and loving, and where

I hardly felt White. Eyes glanced and glared with distrust and suspicion, from the people seated in the booths to people waiting for their food. Nothing about that particular McDonald's felt safe, even in such a beautiful and innocent looking suburb—a symbol of America's deep disconnections near its epicenter, national traumas that stretch back generations.

Don't get me wrong; downtown St. Louis has its charms, but it's *tiny*. St. Louis' problem is a microcosm for what ails the rest of America today: people are completely disconnected from each other. Unlike New York City, where everyone rides the same subway, the whole St. Louis area is an archipelago of small townships. St. Louis has nearly *ninety* small townships; it's not one big metropolitan city. Each little township had its own governance, such as city councils and mayors, and police departments. The area had *fifty-eight police departments*. Many of the townships popped up during the decades of "white flight" from downtown during the postwar era, after the automobile made commuting (and separation) increasingly possible.

While Ferguson seemed tranquil and lovely that morning, there was obviously something completely broken beneath the surface and the system used to govern the place. For starters, in a town that was nearly 70% Black, the police force and city administrators were mostly White. In order to generate revenues, residents got fined for almost everything, including parking violations, court fees, as well as housing code violations, like not taking proper care of your yard according to certain standards. In a city with a population of about 21,000 people, there were roughly 16,000 outstanding arrest warrants, often for minor violations. Although Black residents made up less than 70% of the population, Blacks represented 85% of all traffic stops, 90% of traffic citations, and 93% of the arrests by the Ferguson Police Department between 2012 and 2014. Of the fifty-three commissioned police officers in Ferguson, only three were Black.

What was going on in Ferguson was bullshit. Imagine living in a place where you got fined all the time and lived in fear of getting warrants placed on you. Well, that's how many of Ferguson's residents felt.

It was difficult to comprehend the depth of the roots of the disconnection. One older Black man, a professor, was on the bus when we got back from McDonald's. He explained how for many Blacks in Missouri, the term "sheriff" goes back to the slavery era. The police, therefore, merely conjured up a painful system of Black oppression. Although I grew up as the son of a judge with sheriff's officers who were pillars of the community, the deep distrust for law enforcement made a lot more sense in St. Louis and Missouri generally—a state that has never governed itself seeing all people as "one."

Later, as we drove out of town, the professor pointed out the Target parking lot that the Missouri National Guard used as a staging area, and as I looked out the right window, there was the entrance to Emerson Electric, the Fortune 500 engineering and technology company. *Holy shit*, I thought, looking at the gleaming, manicured lawns paving the way to a security gate. Emerson Electric was yet another corporate island, detached from its community. Later, I did some checking and found that Emerson took pride in going on like business as usual during the upheaval. It was all starting to add up.

America may be a very religious country, but it's not a very spiritual one. Unlike wisdom from many spiritual traditions, we don't really think of being "one" on a shared human quest. Instead, too many of us live more in our fears than our dreams, feeling as though no one really has our back, and most everyone ends up feeling quite alone. It's as if we've forgotten why we're all here in the first place, or never imagined what's possible if we're all living our best selves together.

Ferguson turned out to be the canary in the coal mine. It was a crucial microcosm to understand: fear breeds fear and disconnection breeds disconnection. What gave me hope was that Uncle Joe and Aunt Liz agreed that feeling that enormous lack of safety and belonging in Ferguson was bullshit. They too felt alone every day, like no one had their back. The emotional undercurrents in rural and urban America were similar, but the central problem seemed to be that the country was so disconnected, it was hard for people to understand each other's human experiences and realities.

Down the street from the McDonald's on West Florissant Avenue, Harold, the composer and pianist in our group, and Patrick, our filmmaker, found a barber shop called The Final Cut, and Harold sat in a chair for a clean-up. They were joined by Aidan McAuley, who lived on the other side of St. Louis in University City, a relatively wealthy and diverse neighborhood that borders Washington University. In each city where we stopped, we had local "shepherds" to guide us, and Aidan was one of them in St. Louis. People came out of the woodwork from all parts of town to visit with us—a reminder of just how many self-identified Black Sheep were out there.

Aidan was a salesman by day, and by night his passion was to bring more creativity into America's education system. Approaching his 40th birthday, and the father of three girls, Aidan was part of a group of four dads called The Montessori Madmen, who fervently believed that more kids should experience Montessori-style education—a learning system that espouses self-directed learning that follows kids' interests and curiosity. The Madmen all had day jobs, then pursued their cause and passion at night. They had a website and swag and everything. The Montessori Madmen too seemed to be on a mission from God to bring more creativity into America's education system. Like Danny, they could have climbed aboard the Glitter Bus and joined us without missing a beat. It was inspiring. These were just a couple of the countless people who gave me real hope for the country, and for humanity itself.

The owner of the barber shop, Courtney, was another person who gave me hope. He had been sitting outside it, finishing a cigarette, which he did even as he held the front door open for us. He was probably trying to figure out who the hell these guys were: Patrick, Aidan, and Harold. Harold was there for his trim, Aidan sat quietly in the background, and Patrick was filming everything. As Harold moved towards the barber chair, he explained how he was part of a group of artists and entrepreneurs traveling around America.

"You, by living here, have an understanding," Patrick explained. "You own your business, and you're doing some interesting stuff with your life. You have your perspective on things, and that's what we're looking for: people who have a unique perspective, and are doing interesting things with their life."

Courtney nodded, inhaled a large puff, then walked back inside the front door as he threw the cigarette butt outside.

"Yeah," he replied, looking down as he smiled. He exhaled, and had a look of pride while saying, "Whew! Talk about *chance*."

He seemed satisfied by what he was hearing, and came back over to the chair where Harold was seated.

"Tell me your name again?" Harold asked, extending his hand for a clasp.

"It's Courtney," the owner replied, clasping Harold's hand.

"This is Patrick," Harold said. Patrick had his camera trained on Harold and Courtney.

"What's up, Patrick," Courtney uttered, as he grabbed an electric razor and started buzzing the hair on Harold's neck.

Courtney's young daughter, no more than two years old, sat on an older girl's lap in the back of the shop.

"I left her last night at 11:00 and got here this morning at 6:00," he said with a sweet grin, as he surveyed Harold's head and the job to be done.

"How'd you get into cuttin' hair?" Harold asked after Courtney took a break trimming his beard.

"Actually, uh . . . I started cutting my own hair when I was 11 years old," he replied as he smiled at the memory. "I had a barber and he messed my hair up. I didn't like the haircut so I went home and cut it all off and said I was never going to another barber shop again!"

It was the first gig he ever had, and it might as well have been his last. After trying painting and construction, he came back to hair. After being arrested for cocaine possession (what apparently later tested as ibuprofen), he did a stint in prison, and then started his own barber shop.

This, however, wasn't what was uppermost on Harold's mind. "Some people like to push my hairline," Harold said, pointing upwards with his index finger, then turned to look up at Courtney. "People do this thing where they try to get you to look like Steve Harvey and stuff—pushing your hairline back."

"Right, right," Courtney replied, then turned Harold's chair towards the mirror, a serious look on his face. "You think it's back? Did I push it back?"

"No, no, no! You're doing good!" Harold chimed, "I'm just paranoid. I'm kinda traumatized."

Both chuckled, then started settling into Courtney's story. He described growing up in the St. Louis area, about twenty minutes from the barber shop.

"They call me the black sheep a lot!" Courtney shared with a laugh, combing Harold's head.

Harold almost couldn't believe his ears. "That is so funny that they call you the black sheep because remember how I told you I'm traveling with this group of artists and entrepreneurs? What do you think the name of the group is?" He reacted in such a way that Courtney held up his comb, waiting.

"The Black Sheep?" Courtney replied calmly.

"How'd you know that?" Harold asked quickly, sounding amazed.

"Uh, you know . . . " Courtney said with a big toothy grin, "Put it together."

"Yep," Harold replied with a chuckle.

"But I think a lot of people feel like black sheep!"

It felt like Courtney was one of us.

Aidan beamed quietly in the back, knowing already that this was a special day that he would never forget.

Courtney's mom who worked two jobs, and Courtney was the middle of three children. His mom had a stroke when he was nine, and his younger brother had issues.

"So Mom didn't really worry about you in that way. I mean, she was busy," Harold continued in his characteristic engaging way. "You're here right now, so that says to me you were able to take care of yourself."

"Yeah . . . yeah . . . I learned to survive."

In the mirror behind Courtney, we could see his daughter, still sitting in the lap of the young girl who was doing her hair. The toddler was dressed in pink and occasionally cooing.

"It kinda left me out in limbo," Courtney continued, saying he spent a lot of time with his relatives, or living on the streets.

"How did you feel then, about all that stuff?" Harold probed.

"At the time, I was kind of numb to it all," Courtney replied, leaning back with his comb as he beamed another wide smile. "You know, if I started doing this when I was *nineteen*, man, I'd be *set* by now!"

"So that numbness you were talking about with your feelings," Harold continued, channeling his inner Oprah. "If you were capable of feeling that stuff, and sitting with yourself in that way, how different do you think things would have been?"

"Well, I think my biggest issue was that I used to kinda *trip* off what my family thought—you know, what other people thought of me."

"I know what that's like!" Harold perked.

"Now, if you try to please everybody and the more you try to please them, the less they're satisfied," he paused for a moment, "Mmm . . ."

Harold listened intently, interjecting "rights" and "uh-huhs" here and there, as Courtney continued to open up—almost as if he was talking with an old friend.

By then, Aidan was completely absorbed by the conversation. For Aidan, it was all about his being able to connect with Courtney without fear. Although they lived on different sides of St. Louis and were different races, Aidan felt a kinship with Courtney the more he listened to the barber speak. Perhaps it was that they were both fathers of daughters. Perhaps it was Courtney's gentle nature, or his willingness to be vulnerable. For some reason, Aidan thought about the documentary *My Life as a Turkey*, about a man who raised wild turkeys and then walked with them into nature. When the man was with the turkeys in nature, the deer and other wildlife trusted him and didn't run away. They could all feel more connected. The same was true for Aidan in the back of the barber shop; he felt completely connected with Harold and Courtney.

At one point, Harold asked, "What was the hardest thing you've been through?"

Courtney immediately recalled when his grandmother told him and his brothers that they couldn't stay at their house anymore. His mom was in rehab and the banks had been coming around, so they were going to lose the house. Courtney's older brother went to his girlfriend's house, while his younger brother went to stay at the grandmother's. Courtney stayed at his mom's house. When he got home from school the next day, the bank had boarded it up.

"Man, that day we had one of these real bad thunderstorms. It was one of the worst hail storms St. Louis had in the '80s. And, I was stuck outside. Man, I didn't have nowhere to go."

Harold stared intently down at the floor as Courtney shaved his neck.

"So that was just when we had got these dumpsters, and there wasn't nowhere for me to go!" he said, leaning back. "And I will never get out of my head the sound of that hail hitting that dumpster. *It sounded like death in there, man!*"

"Hmm . . ." Harold hummed, without moving.

"Like I say, *I was a kid*, and when you're young, you think you got all these safety nets, and the world is all one way, you know . . ."

"How old were you then?"

"I was eleven years old," he continued, "It was crazy. I didn't have nowhere to go that day. But I think that was about the worst incident I can remember. I mean, I've had other incidents that were far worse, thank you, but that's the one that shook me up!"

Aidan would never forget that story. Just imagining Courtney as a little boy seeking shelter in a dumpster choked him up even years later. It was almost an unimaginable circumstance for him, who lived in a four-bedroom house on a beautiful street in University City. He was blown away by Courtney's resilience.

As Harold's haircut wrapped up, Aidan was so moved that he asked if he could give Courtney a hug. Courtney didn't hesitate, and the two made plans to get together again soon. They ended up developing a sweet friendship. Aidan brought Courtney a new water filter, especially mindful of Courtney's newborn, while Courtney trimmed Aidan's hair.

Aidan, Harold—neatly trimmed, with his hairline just right—and Patrick returned to the bus feeling a sense of inspiration about the connection they had just made. They had found another Black Sheep! Aidan seemed elated, seeing his own city through a new lens. It inspired all of us, just witnessing their energy, including Cowboy, our bus driver from Oklahoma with a handlebar mustache. Aidan was good like that; he was one of the countless Americans—"shepherds," we called them—we met on tour who were characterized by their respect, decency, and generosity.

People like Aidan opened their hearts and homes to us. Quite literally. Feeling great pride as hosts in their city, Aidan and his family moved out of their house and stayed at his mother's for a few nights to let us stay in his. With the Glitter Bus parked out on the tree-lined street, a few neighbors came by to see what was going on. Harold played the piano in Aidan's living room, and neighbors and friends of Aidan's and the other "shepherds" came by. Patrick shot videos in front yards, capturing local voices. It was all informal and relaxed. Sleeping in kids' beds and surrounded by toys, we felt like we were part of a much larger family, sharing a feeling of love and belonging that we all cherished.

This was perhaps our greatest observation about the America we encountered on tour: that it was doing a hell of a lot better than the media or political narratives made things out to be. Out in the grassroots, politics rarely came up.

That generosity of spirit and hospitality is a part of America you can feel and experience if you're able to look at the country and people with curiosity and openness. Like those who travel the world and realize that people everywhere are more similar than different, the same is true in America.

Sitting in the back of the Glitter Bus, reflecting about America, it struck me again and again: America is such a complex place, as complex as humanity itself. The country is impossible to characterize in a few simple words. America's level of diversity and complexity means that not everyone will know and sing the same songs, or feel a sense of belonging. Too often, no one felt like they belonged! That said, out of America's remarkable diversity emerged one of the most innovative and productive economies and civilizations in history.

The greatest challenge for America, it seemed, was to bridge the human disconnection and create a culture where people felt like they belonged at a time when there were a lot of forces pulling us apart, especially politics.

The good news was that the picture of America on the ground was far better than the sometimes vapid, angry culture the media portrayed. Sure, the country was having a crisis. But the nature and extent of the crisis wasn't what we were interested in. The question we asked quite a bit was whether America might be ready to go through a moral revival—a renaissance if you will. The answer to that question, we concluded, would not come from some politician on a white horse. The answer will depend on you. And me. And all of us, stepping into our voices, our agency, and our humanity—our inner artists if you will—and *deciding that we are going to do things differently.*

How to start on that journey?

It is often through our greatest vulnerabilities, not our successes, that we connect most deeply with each other, which reminds us what it is to be human. And our visit to Ferguson pushed toward the front of my mind a thought: art. Art might be the means of easiest connection. Art, after all, was our fastest, most available means of transcendence. A song sung, an image sketched, a photograph taken, a story told, however it is told.

Just as Aidan felt bonded for life to Courtney, Danny shared with the Black Sheep his anxiety, while Harold shared some of the addictions from his past. We connected on a deep level, not just a wise sage and a mentee, but as people relating through pains, feelings of shame and self-doubt, aspirations too, and, well, their art. The wounds and less savory parts of us make us human, ignite our art, and help us realize that we're much more similar than different. Waves of hopelessness and helplessness hit Uncle Joe and Aunt Liz as much as they had Danny, Harold, Courtney. The emotional experience of being in rural and urban America had many commonalities, even if politicians on all sides often exploited those emotions, pitting us against one another.

Although it would be a year before Danny started painting, we would be there for him when he did. Keeping in touch through social media, Danny started live painting on Facebook, and although there were only a few people watching, Harold and I were among them and we were struck by his enormous talent. After reconnecting with him and hearing Danny's dreams, we called up Aidan, who started spending time with Danny on a regular basis. Aidan helped Danny set up an LLC, drove him and his artwork around town to prospective patrons, and helped Danny get out of debt. Before long, Danny was harnessing the patrons we knew to sell his paintings for tens of thousands of dollars, and he got himself a scholarship to art school in San Francisco. Danny and Aidan became friends for life.

The tour over, this is what I saw (and felt). *We* are the leaders we have been waiting for. We can connect through our shadows and vulnerabilities, being courageous enough to be human, and lift each other up rather than tear each other down. Our heroes are people like Aidan and Courtney (and Danny). And art was just the Trojan Horse, our way to get under the hood of the human and emotional experience in America, a country that surely needed an artistic renaissance. Thank God for art—one of the great bridges humanity has to connect and imagine a richer life together.

One thing was clear: the country looked a hell of a lot better when you got out into it than it did from watching it on television. We were taken with the generosity of spirit we encountered everywhere, from strangers even, the type of values that fueled Giving Tuesday to new heights each year. It all begged us to ask time and again what price we all pay when so much of our lives shifted towards our screens, large and small, and away from real connection. Perhaps it's the price we must all pay for living inside a system that rewards preying upon our fears and traumas. We've allowed our widely accepted and preached versions of success to dehumanize us all.

There was only one way out of all that, as best I could figure. Every one of us has to make a choice: do we let the system turn us into helpless automatons and victims, or do we summon the courage to look into our traumas, do some hard personal work, and seek to reinvent our lineage?

None of us can do that alone. Just ask Uncle Joe.

CHAPTER ELEVEN

BACK INTO THE WOODS

"Let's get back to being human," Uncle Joe said in a tone equal parts prayer and plea for relief. It was a phrase he had used before, another classic Uncle Joe-ism, and it hit home.

That morning began at 3:45 a.m. with a part of me feeling like a kid again. I was outside my aunt and uncle's house, almost as familiar to me as my own, and beside it was not just its most familiar feature but the reason I was awake so very early: an eighteen-wheeler logging truck. "Lorang Logging— Dutch Flat, California" was painted in red cursive on Uncle Joe's truck door.

A few moments later, a side door to the house opened and Uncle Joe shuffled out, unable to conceal his age. His body tilted a few degrees off center like the Tower of Pisa. He dragged one foot after the other, just a bit, not quite limping towards his truck. Gone were his strong shoulders and the seeming invincibility that I remembered from my youth, yet he was still one of my heroes.

"Mornin'," he said with mild enthusiasm, clearly still waking up and snorting to clear his nose as he walked across the driveway.

"Morning!" I jabbered, by then having been wide-awake for nearly an hour. Rides in Uncle Joe's truck were one of the highlights of my youth. He'd even bring his truck to my birthday parties and give my friends and me a ride, horn blaring. Although we were both much older, some of that joyous expectation crept into my mind.

After tossing his Thermos of coffee and a small cooler containing his lunch into the cab, he climbed up into the driver's bucket seat and started up the engine, mumbling as few words as possible and still sniffling. And then we pulled out of the driveway and into the thickly-wooded mountain darkness.

As he shifted gears over and over again, the engine responded with revving and power. And as he repeatedly turned that giant wheel back and forth, slight groans leaked out from his mouth, defying his near-zealous stoicism. It was hard to fathom that he had been doing this job for over forty years—and with little hope of retirement in sight. Most people I knew in New York and Silicon Valley would quit their jobs if they had to routinely wake up at 3 a.m. It's hard to feel human when you're living paycheck to paycheck, mostly focused on survival.

The hardest thing Aunt Liz and Uncle Joe had experienced lately, though, had little to do with the economy. They lost a child—one of the most painful, difficult things any parent can experience.

It had been over three years since their daughter Jennie had passed away tragically, but still Aunt Liz would choke up, swallow gulps of pain, and cry when she thought about Jennie. Seeing Aunt Liz experience such pain and recurring trauma was agonizing. She and Jennie had been best friends and had talked pretty much every day. And in the tiny town of Dutch Flat, where everyone knew everyone, the news of Jennie's sudden death shocked the whole town.

At the memorial service at the Dutch Flat Hotel held a few days after her death, Uncle Joe wore sunglasses to shield his swollen eyes, and his whole body seemed numb with emotion. When the time came for him to say a few words, he asked me to read comments he had typed up. His words were brief, remembering Jennie, yet he also had a message. He hoped some of the people gathered that day, especially the younger ones, might learn from Jennie's alcoholism and not drive drunk. Perhaps some meaning could be excavated from tragedy, his words suggested. But his pain and the trauma of a daughter's death ran deeper than I could have known at the time.

The guilt that Uncle Joe would feel for years following Jennie's death was silent yet palpable: had she developed her alcoholism from his role modeling? After all, he'd had a few beers after work every day and he had been working over forty years. And that wasn't counting weekends. What could he have done differently? What change might have saved Jennie's life?

Guilt is one of the most powerful emotions. It lurks in shadows, sometimes for years, sometimes for generations, oppressing the human spirit and chaining the soul. As if that smoldering guilt alone weren't enough of a burden, it rarely comes alone. Not far behind were two other emotions: hopelessness and despair.

After following the headlights around winding dirt roads for nearly two hours, glimmers of sunlight started to dance through the dense forest, pirouetting between the shadowed silhouettes. As we made it to the top of a ridge, the true magnificence of the day announced itself. Surrounded by broad swaths of lush forest and meadows as far as the eye could see, the greenery of Northern California, about an hour north and east of Sacramento to be precise, was interrupted by only sparkling granite, ponds, and lakes.

"Wow! What a day!" I exclaimed with child-like wonder.

"Oh, man!" he replied with a nod and boyish grin, before cracking his window to invite in the crisp mountain air.

"Imagine, Uncle Joe," I bantered, slipping into my smart-ass mode that he was all too familiar with, "you could be headed to work in an office right now!"

Pausing only for dramatic effect, and with a sneer worthy of a trademark, Uncle Joe looked off at the gorgeous view that stretched for miles and exclaimed, "I've got the best corner office in the world!"

His grin was wide, warm, and authentic. And taking in that view, it was impossible to argue the point. He did in fact have the best corner office in the world.

Moments like these, when he was enveloped in nature, were Uncle Joe's heaven on Earth. If you didn't spend a day with him in his truck, you might not understand this about him, hidden beneath the stoicism, wit, intelligence, and, well, dirt. But make no mistake: Uncle Joe's humanity ultimately resided in what Henry David Thoreau celebrated as the "absolute freedom and wildness" of nature. Like Uncle Joe, Thoreau relished being immersed in nature for its earnestness, its sincerity, and its strength. As Thoreau put it, "live deep and suck out all the marrow of life."

From that corner office, Uncle Joe surveyed a vast common richness, all that wealth of nature. For decades, he had worked with others to both put food on his table and provide the raw materials used to make tables, houses, and damn near everything else. We were off to pick up the first load of logs.

I was in that cab, enjoying that view, but I had known for a long time that something wasn't right; something was misfiring for my aunt and uncle, something surrounding the tragedy and trials of their lives. I had seen it in Uncle Joe. After years of hope for change, the signs of cynicism were creeping in. Uncle Joe yelled more at "idiot" drivers or passersby on the freeway. He worried about paying for things and taking care of his family, seeing that the people he knew and cared for were in fact cared for. And increasingly he resented knowing that hedge-fund managers and traders still made millions, perhaps on trades on the trees he had logged. Mainly, he hoped that my generation would step up more because he was losing hope watching the "money whores" in Washington, DC and on Wall Street. Even though he leaned more conservative, the Occupy Wall Street protests resonated with him: why should the top 1% have so much—so much more power, so much more wealth, so much royal treatment—in *America*?

America had birthed a new aristocracy: an aristocracy of capital.

Alexis de Tocqueville and Uncle Joe could certainly have an interesting chinwag about money. It's easy to forget that for centuries Europe was dominated by a handful of feudal landowners toward whom "the people" routinely summed up anger and courage enough to occasionally take on, sometimes executing a few, sometimes more than a few, in the case of the American and

French Revolutions. Through the Enlightenment in the 17th and 18th centuries, the people actually clawed back some of their wealth and power. Philosophers like Adam Smith, John Locke, and de Tocqueville elevated science, rationalism, capitalism, and democracy as a way for individuals to break free from the landed aristocracy. It was a curiosity the Frenchman brought to America when he came to study the young republic. Journeying from town to town, Tocqueville saw money-making as the great liberator of American individualism and an engine for social equality 160 years before Shawn Carter left The Marcy Projects to become Jay-Z.

But capitalism as a liberating force for innovation, solving problems, abundance, and leveling by talent, luck, and risk-taking had somewhere in the late-twentieth century become something else. Entrepreneurial capitalism got upstaged in many ways by finance capitalism, and American capitalism became "financialized." The hedge-fund managers, LBO dorks, and their ilk held increasing amounts of financial, political, and social power.

The talent and the money flowed increasingly to the financial wizards whom I worked with in London or New York, those who had mastered the art of harnessing assets to produce more capital. Regular people like Uncle Joe lost. From 1979 to 2019, the bottom 90% of wage earners in America saw their income increase by just 26%. During the same time period, wage-earners in the top 0.1% grew 345%. Today, the share of overall wealth between the top 0.1% and the bottom 90% is roughly the same, comparable to levels of inequality in the late 1920s before the Great Depression.

The American Dream became increasingly distant for most people. While 90% of people born in the 1940s ended up with higher income distribution than their parents, only 40% of people born in 1980 have done so. We are still processing the effects of globalization and a technology revolution, as well as the corrosive effects of all that money chasing more money inside our institutions. Given that context, it's easier to understand the record levels of distrust of government and business, and why Uncle Joe felt increasingly agonized and hopeless.

"Money whores" and a culture of greed was how Uncle Joe explained it. The whole system was full of "goddamn money whores." Well, maybe insecure, overachieving "money whores" who just need a bit of love, and who used wealth as a scorecard and to validate self-worth, but point taken. In urban and rural America, and pretty much all parts in between, money is the à la mode. It's the investor's and the rapper's delight, as much as it is also the logger's plight.

That was it: money for money's sake had become as American as baseball and apple pie.

After we picked up the first load of logs, we were gunning down another logging road by the time I prodded him again.

"So . . . if you had ten minutes with President Obama, what would you say to him?" I asked.

"With Obama? Ahh, shit. I don't know . . ."

"You voted for him."

"Yeah, well . . . he's all right. But tell you what: *both* sides have kicked the can down the road and *damn near over a cliff*!"

We both laughed, like old times, bonded by laughter.

The mill we were headed for was about thirty minutes away and it was time for some music. Uncle Joe's soundtrack of life was classic rock, and Aunt Liz bought him a satellite-radio system so he could listen to it all day. One of his favorite songs ever,

Sympathy for the Devil by The Rolling Stones, *just happened* to come on.

Every now and then, it does seem like the universe acts with purpose. For as we drove towards the mill entrance, Uncle Joe wanted to talk about one of his pet topics, those devilish money whores, though not with much sympathy. He had a broad definition for what characterized a "money whore" that included many politicians as well as greedy people who sought to benefit themselves at the expense of others. His passion made sense. It was obvious to everyone in the family that Uncle Joe's cynicism increased quite a bit following the Great Recession of '08-'09, and this was about five years later. As we drove inside the mill grounds, surrounded by acres of giant piles of logs as we edged towards two giant loaders that added to those piles by unloading a line of truck trailers, Uncle Joe, who was always good with math, broke it down.

"I make about thirty percent less these days," he said. That was the toll of the recession and its aftermath: a third less buying power for the same hours worked.

"Geez, that's a lot," I replied, not having realized the extent of the re-set.

"It's the money whores!" he said, looking at me with an unusual intensity emanating from his blue eyes. "It's all a bunch o' money whores!"

"Say more."

"Okay. Well, . . . you see that load," he said, pointing through the rear window of the cab at the load of logs. "We just drove several hours to pick them up so that some person—or persons— people—can build a house or a fence or . . . *whatever!*"

"Right."

"But I make *less* money per day than I did a few years ago."

"Right."

"So I drive three loads a day now."

"Right."

"I used to drive *two!*"

"Ah. Got it. That explains the sixteen-hour days . . ."

It all seemed too much for someone Uncle Joe's age.

"Meanwhile, some hedge-fund guy or trader—I don't know what you call these guys. You know who these guys are better than me! Anyhow, there's some guy sitting at some *desk* somewhere right now, making a *shitload* of money without actually *making* or *creating anything!*"

Once again, Uncle Joe had a way of nailing things so simply.

"These guys are *trading* the wood that *I hauled* and make *more money* than *anyone* else."

"Right."

"For what?" he asked, sounding plaintive now. "For *what?*"

"Good question," I replied, feeling my blood rise.

"What exactly are *these assholes* doing for the world?"

"Nothing. They are creating *absolutely nothing!*" I cringed, just imagining these guys in their comfortable offices in New York and London.

"Now you're getting with it!" he chided with a grin, slapping my arm, *"Money whores!"*

"Well, they're lucky they're in that safe office and not here now, that's for sure!" I said, laughing.

"We could strap 'em on the back!" Uncle Joe offered, widening his eyes with a mischievous grin, although he barely got the words out before we were howling again.

That was quite a visual: a bunch of commodity traders and

hedge-fund managers and investors strapped to the back of a logging truck going down the highway.

"And they are paying lower tax rates than you, Uncle Joe!" I continued, adding fuel to the fire.

"Oh, man!" he replied with a big grin. "Wrappers. *Wrappers!*" he exhorted, referring to the thick metal cables that hold the logs onto the trailer.

This was the other side, the human side, of the system from London and New York; the other side of the spreadsheets; and, the other side of the ashes from the economic inferno that Dick Fuld and Lehman Brothers and so many others helped ignite. The piles of logs next to loaders driven by a twenty-something young man trying to establish a craft that could pay the bills. The work gloves. The dust. The husband-and-wife team who drove two trucks in a small business whom we passed. Every driver waving at each other or saying a brief hello with a blink of their lights or a quick greeting into their CB radios, often seeking laughs and tonics of connection. Loggers, Uncle Joe explained, have a kinder and closer community than most truck drivers. They stop to help each other if another truck needs an extra cable or breaks down, as I saw Uncle Joe do a number of times, including once when he gave another driver a spare part he just happened to have. Maybe it was their proximity to nature that removed the edge and attitude that other truck drivers sometimes exhibited. Fathers, mothers, and grandfathers even, working hard every day, much harder than I ever did, just to get by. Days that start well before dawn that often bleed into near nightfall with the increased workload.

After a three-load day, only a cold Coors Light and shot of whiskey could ease Uncle Joe's growing aches and pains.

Day in, day out; week in, week out: the process repeats. The feelings of despair masquerade as nihilism, wondering just what this life is all about. Another day; another dollar. But to what end? Duty and principles extend only so far before the political rhetoric resonates more deeply. The despair gives rise to unprecedented levels of addictions. Painkillers. Opioids. Heroin.

The system had given rise to a new aristocracy while leaving almost everyone else behind.

After that, we got to talking about taxes. Naturally, American investors loved the fact that the federal government taxed them just 15%, the capital gains tax rate, on their income from investments. Basic income tax rates, such as Liz and Joe paid, would be much higher—say 28% or more. Who *wouldn't* want that lower rate? But professional investors aren't even usually investing with their own money. Most of the time they risk other peoples' money, and very often other peoples' retirement money. That investment income, called "carried interest," and the different income categorization (investment income, rather than personal income) allowed some of the wealthiest Americans to have a substantially lower tax rate than Uncle Joe.

When the topic of carried interest came up inside my venture capital firm, I saw only one partner argue that the tax laws should be changed to be more fair. For masters of the system, the whole point was to continue to master the system, and that meant paying lower taxes than others. But that one partner isn't alone. The world's most famous investor, Warren Buffett, also couldn't understand the federal government's tax logic. Why should his secretary be paying a higher nominal tax rate on her income than he did on his?

Uncle Joe could hardly take it. In the world of the aristocracy of finance, somehow it was the money whores who were screwing the average guy. Uncle Joe, whom I had always experienced as an optimist and beacon of positivity, was almost visibly bending under waves of both hopelessness and despair.

It would have been hard for me to imagine things getting worse after Jennie's death—until they did. On Christmas Day a few years after the Great Recession hit, it became obvious: my cousin Nick, Joe and Liz's son, was in deep trouble.

My aunt and uncle hosted Christmas at their house every year, and it was always one of Nick's favorite days. It was often Nick who donned the Santa hat to distribute the presents from underneath the tree. That year, however, he disappeared. After nightfall, I noticed Nick's black Honda Civic idling in the drive-way with heavily fogged windows, the headlights on, and music blaring. Nick was inside the car with someone else, although it was so dark, I couldn't tell who. I didn't think too much of it. High school kids.

About fifteen minutes later, Nick came back inside, clearly high as a kite. He was laughing, giddy even. As I looked into his eyes and face, his life flashed before me. His eyes were completely wild, flickering across the room like the fire in the fireplace, and then his smile sent me into shock. As he laughed, most of his front teeth were either jagged or missing.

"Nick, are you okay?" was all I could muster.

"I'm great!" he said, somewhat slurred, "Merry Christmas to all!"

It was that Christmas Day when I internalized that Nick had a serious heroin addiction. He was far from alone. There often wasn't a lot to be hopeful about, at least in terms of thinking about their futures. Nick, still quietly grieving the loss of a sister, found drugs as a way to try to self-medicate.

The family considered an intervention, but before that idea gained momentum Nick checked himself into a Christian recovery program. It was the most courageous thing I had ever seen him do: acknowledging the addiction. Soon he wouldn't be alone in the journey ahead.

Almost the entire family—well, eight people—drove down to see Nick get baptized in the Pacific Ocean. Uncle Joe and my mom recalled it all for me vividly. It was a crisp and clear day at Seacliff State Beach near Santa Cruz on Monterey Bay with temperatures in the low to mid-50s, and wisps of thin white clouds high up in the sky. A fishing pier extended about a hundred yards from the beach, punctuated near the end by the remnants of an old "cement ship," as locals called it. In fact, it was a 430-foot WWI-era tanker that had cascaded into the sand shore one winter night during heavy storms.

Gathering around before the baptism, Uncle Joe had on one of his well-worn flannel shirts and dark blue jeans, as well as his sunglasses, barely hiding his anguish behind his stoic facial expressions. Aunt Liz swallowed back emotion again, casting her ever-loving yet squinted eyes upon her son. The thought of losing *both* children was something Aunt Liz and Uncle Joe had been trying for months to get out of their minds. Nick was dressed as something between a hipster and a punk, with a white checkered hat and hoodie and sunglasses. Yet soon all that armor came off.

Nick would place his fate, and their faith, in God and Jesus Christ. A pastor in his fifties with a shaved head and gray goatee welcomed everyone. There were five other young men, roughly

149

in their late teens, who would join Nick in the ocean. Nick was shocked and moved by how many family members showed up. Aunts and uncles, cousins, and his former girlfriend Krista had made a several-hour drive to support him. (Only one other family member, a sister, showed up for the other four boys combined.) Krista was Nick's high-school sweetheart, at least until he got consumed by drugs. Her love for him was dedicated, patient, and beautiful. Coming from a close-knit and devoted Christian family, Krista had helped Nick get into Teen Challenge, the recovery program.

Just a few weeks into the program, the day of his baptism, Nick looked humble and peaceful. He recorded a short video testimonial about his commitment to Christ, and to the process he had enrolled himself to find sobriety. As the boys stripped down to their swim trunks and walked out towards the water, they gathered in a circle with the pastor in the center, heads bowed in prayer. Nick had a different expression in this moment: a look of determination. His sister's memory was always with him, a fact commemorated by a large tattoo of Jennie's face and the date she passed away on his upper back.

As Nick waded into the ocean with the pastor, deep pain converged with hope and the cold Pacific Ocean waters. It was a seminal moment in his life. The never-ending anguish of losing a sister. The claws of addiction. Lost teeth. Lost friends. Lost identity. Lost girlfriend. Death's door. And yet from some dimly lit corner of Nick's soul, a belief emerged that life could be different. Better. A glimmer of light and love. Krista. His family. Everyone cared. The pastor cared. God and Jesus loved him. After wading waist-deep into the ocean, the pastor held him as Nick fell backwards and doused his head into the ocean.

Holy shit, it's cold! That's what Nick thought, yet this was most definitely a turning point in his life.

When I think back on that day and that moment, zooming out on Nick, those boys, and that beach, with the old cement shipwreck in the background, the song *Everyday Life* by Coldplay comes into mind and heart.

Nick had surrendered, and perhaps found himself by doing so.

All of this—Jennie and Nick, the way the world could stack up against most of the humans in it—were in that cab with Uncle Joe and me. And despite the many reasons to be cynical about the American Dream, reasons that would propel Donald Trump's future run for the Presidency—I'll never forget what Uncle Joe said next.

"We have to realize that we are the boss, not victims or helpless," he enthused, ratcheting up his voice. "We have forgotten who's in charge. *We are the goddamn boss!*"

"Now *that* is an inspiring thought!" I responded enthusiastically, "You see, Uncle Joe, this is precisely why President Obama needs to hear your voice."

"Yeah, well," he uttered, looking off into nature, seeming to want to calm down and change the subject.

Uncle Joe said what even the silver-tongued Tocqueville might not have been able to say. It was a rallying cry for the times, especially when so many felt so helpless and powerless. People didn't feel represented, let alone human, and pretty much everyone seemed to feel about the same way.

He wrapped up his impassioned rant, with what could be a chant: "If something isn't working, you usually try something else!"

"Hell, yes!"

We both knew this is why we spent so much time talking.

"I tell you what," he said, "These are your problems now, not mine! I'm too goddamn old and tired."

"Don't throw in the towel just yet," I said, convinced if not convincing. "It's gonna get interesting."

꙳

It was about a year after Nick checked into rehab when he and Harold met. It was a night none of us saw coming. After Nick had finished the intensive portion of the rehabilitation program in Watsonville, California, not far from that beach near Monterey where he had accepted Christ, his Savior, he headed back up north to the mountains and began the final portion of the program. Nick landed at the Sierra Woods Lodge, a quaint fourteen-room motor lodge owned by Teen Challenge. It looked for all the world like what it had been, a modest hotel tucked into the scenic beauty of the California Sierra mountains. If you happened to pull over, you probably wouldn't know that the staff was running a rehab, unless you tried to order a beer in the cafe or restaurant.

The lodge itself was set against a gorgeous backdrop including a meadow in front of a plush, tree-covered ridge. The dozen or so young men in the program slept in one large basement room lined with bunkbeds beneath the lodge. It smelled like a gym, though everything was neat and tidy down there. While there were always challenging moments, the group largely acted like a brotherhood or family, seeking out ways to support each other. They woke up each morning, between 5:30 and 6:00 a.m., and began each day with a devotional and prayer in the cafe at 6:30.

By the time Nick reached Sierra Woods, he was a completely different person than the year before. He was committed to his faith and to honoring Jesus and the Lord. He had a new evangelical quality to him. It wasn't just that he wanted to persuade people about the merits of faith and God, as he did with Uncle Joe and Aunt Liz. He also shared his story of transformation from drug addiction as a testimonial in hopes that it might inspire others.

The difference was clear, and I could imagine how relieved Uncle Joe and Aunt Liz felt that Nick was coming back.

It was Aunt Liz who suggested that while Harold was in town we go visit Nick and the lodge. After all, it was open to the public. And it would be good for me to see Nick and witness his progress.

Harold and I looked forward to going, and drove there with Uncle Joe and a couple of others. It was dark and fairly cold out by the time we arrived but the cafe was warm and cozy. Next to the cafe was a small pellet stove burning next to an old brown Cline upright piano pushed against the wall. Since word had spread among the young men that a great pianist would visit them that night, they had gathered in the cafe by the time we arrived. It was as if George Gershwin had come to town, bringing with him a welcome change of scenery.

As soon as Harold walked in, something about the lodge felt familiar to him. Nick greeted us at the door and gave us the nickel tour. He showed us the restaurant and introduced us to the supervisors and some of his colleagues. The more Nick spoke, the more Harold's body language seemed to relax and warm, almost as if Harold felt at home. It was actually deeper than that. Something about the lodge felt *sacred* to Harold, for reasons only he could understand at that moment. Uncle Joe,

Nick, and I would learn why only years later, but just watching the change in his features, his posture, the ease of his being in that place, all helped explain what happened next.

You see, coming from entirely different parts of America, Harold, Nick, and the boys in that lodge were connected deeply by one of their greatest vulnerabilities.

Harold couldn't have put it into words at that moment, but he too had struggled with addiction. Turns out, Harold went through his own reinvention and rehabilitation eight years prior when he went through two years of intensive personal growth to transform himself from addiction. Marijuana had been Harold's addiction, and the young men reminded him of the people he had done his recovery work with. The grounded sobriety of the lodge comforted him.

Things came to a brink for Harold in New York City. Back then, Harold was already a successful jazz performer, yet he was dirt poor. After his dad became disabled, Harold struggled to live in the city. Marijuana became a crutch, and Harold, compulsive about everything, turned to it so much that it started to affect every aspect of his life. His career stagnated, he was in a dysfunctional relationship, and he was depressed. One night, even after the euphoria of winning a karate competition, Harold wanted to kill himself. Fortunately, his karate teacher had been there and talked him out of it.

Thankfully, Harold found a group in Colorado with whom he could do the work of emotional growth. Over a two-year period, Harold got sober, and worked through a number of traumas from his past.

Now, when visiting Nick we didn't know any of this. But by the time Harold sat down at that upright piano and started playing the music, the vibe *felt* different. After I briefly introduced him, he played *Marvelous Fantasy*, the title track from his latest album. Everyone was transfixed. Some moved to Harold's left or right to be able to see his fingers moving up and down the keys. Like usual, Harold closed his eyes, and seemed to allow the spirits to enter his body as he swayed back and forth, as his body followed the music, as he pressed pedals here and there. The whole room felt like it was levitating along with the rhythms and the riffs, along with Harold.

"There was just something different about that night," is how Uncle Joe put it years later.

It was a magical moment, a moment in life when everyone in the room felt deeply connected to something beyond themselves, and connected to each other. The beaming young men looked joyous, yet they remained attentive and deeply respectful. Of the joy. The connectedness. The humanity in that room. Imagining all the struggles the boys had experienced for years, and how much they deserved a moment like that, caused emotions to well up inside me. Harold knew their struggles better than any of us and he understood: *our struggles are the same.*

After Harold played and the room applauded through a standing ovation, he fielded a few questions before one of the boys, holding sheet music, moved to Harold's right and indicated that he also wanted to play.

"I can't wait to hear you!" Harold encouraged him. Berto, short for Alberto, beamed.

You could tell that hearing Harold's encouragement made Berto's day. He was shorter than the other boys, yet his energetic presence sparkled and he was known for his musical talents. He couldn't stop smiling as he placed the sheet music on the piano.

As Berto's fingers went across the keyboard, the whole room seemed to know what he was playing. It was considered a theme song of sorts at the lodge, a hymn called *Redeemed* by the Christian band Big Daddy Weave.

Bodies swayed, including Harold's, and the boys hummed along. I did too. It was another moment that illustrated that when you peel away this country's tribalism, which cynical opportunists utilize to enhance their own power and profits, the emotional under-belly of urban and rural America have more commonalities than differences. Harold O'Neal, who grew up in public housing in Kansas City, shared the same vulnerabilities as Cousin Nick from the rural hills of Northern California. But there was abundance here too, in caring and compassion. It was another reminder that genuine connection comes not from envy-inducing successes, competitive me-ver-sus-them, but from sharing our commonalities, including our vulnerabilities, including the addictions, traumas, and pains that affect us all. That's where the real growth opportunities and healing reside.

It was a night when vastly different worlds managed to come together and uplift each other. Standing over by the front entrance, Uncle Joe and I took in the remarkable moment. He was choking up, a tear in his left eye tracing a line down his nose and cheek and chin.

Uncle Joe turned to me and said, "That right there . . . That's *love*."

CHAPTER TWELVE

ON THE
ROAD AGAIN

She was the perfect carriage for us, that vintage Willie Nelson band bus. The second Black Sheep bus tour, which launched in Huntington, West Virginia, in the spring of 2018 was already underway for nearly a week when I flew into Pittsburgh to meet up with it. There she was, parked out front of my hotel, with a destination sign that read On the Road Again.

There was something about getting back out on the road again that invigorated the soul, and that bus was built to convey energized souls. She was a 1983 Eagle named Me & Paul, a gift from Willie to his drummer Paul English (who would pass on in 2020), a moving tribute to a beautiful collaboration and best friendship.

Willie Nelson, of course, qualified as an ultimate black sheep. Born in 1933, he's a true artist who has never lost his authentic voice or his gift of making endless artistic contributions to

America and the world, all while having shitloads of fun. That was us, in a nutshell. We wanted to be a part of an artistic and creative renaissance in America at a time when culture has become so "I" centric that most people lose track of themselves and what is important. We were interested in the "we" connective tissue that ultimately holds us all together, the "we" spirit that had helped places like Pittsburgh to transform, the "we" captured by the beautiful music that Willie and Paul made.

It was glorious and sunny on the morning that I saw Me & Paul parked before that hotel. It all fit. Far from a shattered industrial graveyard, Pittsburgh's downtown was beautiful, with terrific restaurants and cultural offerings like ballet, opera, live music, museums like the Warhol, and art galleries. Originally built on the wealth of coal and steel, industries that had cratered since the 1970s, the city had completely reinvented itself over the past several decades, around thriving technology, robotics, and healthcare industries. What's more, there were a lot of passionate Black Sheep in Pittsburgh. Everywhere we went, down one creative corridor after another, people knew about us and shared our passion for the American entrepreneurial and creative renewal we saw emerging from the bottom up.

If Pittsburgh could come back from the dead to thrive once again, we thought, then so could Cleveland and Detroit, New Orleans and Ferguson. And establishing strong "we" cultures was the only way these cities stood a shot at reinventing themselves.

It all clicked, and as far as I was concerned, Me & Paul was now our official bus because we couldn't think of a better vessel to facilitate what we were trying to do. At a time when America was so completely disconnected, she was our magic carpet, a safe human space, where anyone and everyone—regardless of their race, religion, political views, or class—could come inside and just be human and *belong*. It was the opposite of the Tower of Babel; no matter who you were or how you spoke, if you were willing to be human, we understood each other. We were all about people, not politics, something we had to remind ourselves over and over again. Because we were all about belonging.

We encountered that same thirst for belonging, which seemed at the root of what people all around America needed, everywhere. Whether it was outside a rural Walmart, a wealthy suburban school, or inside a city, Me & Paul ignited imaginations and relaxed perceived differences. The bus was more than just our chariot; it was our vessel for connecting with people. "Come aboard," we offered to hundreds of people. Truck drivers at truck stops; construction workers at lunch inside bars; Amish people next to their carriages; entrepreneurs or social entrepreneurs everywhere; and musicians of all stripes. Everyone reacted just about the same: with a smile and, usually, a sense of wonder and playfulness. It was as if the music or imagining Willie and his pot-smoking band just chilled everyone the hell out and created a human space to just connect.

The bus satiated the thirst people had: to just be human and connect—and *belong*. It didn't seem more complicated than that at the end of the day. Art and the Willie bus were merely the Trojan Horse, a way past all the thick defensive walls the system throws up.

Now, I can't remember if we played the song *On the Road Again* that morning or not—we did often enough during the tour—but we were all excited to get back to Detroit. We came on the first bus tour, and Harold and I even went in the dead of winter one year. What drew us back time and time again was that there was something deeply inspiring about Detroit and its people, a spirit that we didn't recognize from life in San Francisco or New York. Those cities seemed to be places where most everyone was focused on their own success rather than a collective success. Detroit was the opposite.

"Who's in here?" I asked, entering the four-bunk bed area between the front cabin and back cabin.

"Yo," Harold said, pulling back a curtain across the bunk where he was relaxing, listening to music with his large headphones. A small light kept his bunk area lit.

"What's up, brother?" I said, clasping his right hand.

"Hey, man," he replied, "Great to have you!"

"Great to be here . . . on the road again!"

We laughed.

"Is Danny in one of these, too?" I asked, pointing to the cloaked bunk beds.

"Yeah. He's in there," Harold replied, pointing to the middle bunk on the other side. "I think he's asleep."

He was referring to Danny McGinnist Jr. from Ferguson and St. Louis. Three years had passed since that first tour and Danny was no longer a teenager, but he surely nailed that he was a Black Sheep. Not too long after we pulled out of Ferguson, Danny took up painting. Much as he loved making music, it turned out he was a fine artist at heart. And *damn* he was good.

I'll never forget the day we realized. I was exercising in a hotel gym in Santa Monica, scrolling through social media feeds when I saw a live video of Danny painting. He was in his apartment, a fact I surmised because there were boxes of cereal in the background. But that wasn't what really caught my eye. His painting looked really good. I sent Harold a text, asking for a second opinion. Harold agreed the painting was very good. Fully inspired, I sent Danny a message from the gym. And I'll be damned if Danny didn't call me right then. He seemed pretty on top of things.

As Danny explained it over the phone, he was still living pretty much hand-to-mouth, yet had found a passion for painting. He just needed a little hand to lift him up. That helping hand would come from Aidan McCauley, the Black Sheep who sat in the back of the barber shop in Ferguson as Harold got a trim. The next thing we knew, he got himself into art school in San Francisco on scholarship, and was selling his paintings to some of the Black Sheep for $10,000 or $15,000 apiece. Danny even impressed the well-known American painter Kehinde Wiley enough that Wiley flew him to New York and gave him all kinds of advice as well as a custom-made suit for when Danny had his first New York show.

I let Danny sleep.

"Want to come hang out up front for a bit?" I asked Harold. "We've got a few hours to go before Detroit."

"Yeah! Give me two minutes," he replied.

"Cool. See you up there."

It was a beautiful day as Larry, our driver, guided the bus up Interstate 75 north, along Lake Erie and past Monroe into Detroit. It had been about seven years since my first trip in 2011. Back then, just after the Great Recession, and after GM declared its first bankruptcy, the city had faced so many challenges that it seemed it might die. Homelessness and record levels of illiteracy gripped the city, and its neighborhoods looked like war zones. Many commercial buildings were empty, decaying shells with their windows all broken, while many homes stood orphaned, abandoned by those unable to pay their mortgages. By some counts, 70,000 buildings, 31,000 homes, and 90,000 vacant lots were abandoned. Pretty much the only signs of life in 2011 came from a cadre of artists and entrepreneurs acting as catalysts for reinvention.

"Are you ready to be inspired?" I asked Elyse Klaidman, Head of Pixar University, who was seated in the front section of the bus.

"Absolutely!" she replied, wide-eyed, beaming.

Things had all kind of come full-circle when Pixar, the place where we found the name Black Sheep in the first place, sponsored the bus tour. Elyse really made Pixar's sponsorship happen, but Ed Catmull's blessing ensured it. We nicknamed Elise "Luv" because she was one of those people who just radiated a type of easy, calm, unrelenting, maternal love. She took Danny under her wing, and he loved her back. She became Danny's "Mom" on tour while Harold acted like something of a big brother. We worried that the whole leap into new worlds and paydays might overwhelm Danny, so we surrounded him with love and support.

It was time for all of us to go back inside the womb of renewal in America.

⚡

A few minutes past 9 a.m. the day after we arrived in Detroit, we were greeted outside the Russell Industrial Center, that massive,

2.2 million square-foot industrial complex that was more than half a mile long and wider than two football fields, by the unmistakable silhouette of Alan Kaniarz. From the moment we met back in 2011, Alan seemed like he belonged to a different era. Some of it had to do with his long, white mustache and matching goatee, leather cap, and black, horned-rimmed glasses. But it was more than that. It was as if Alan's soul was trapped in the late 1800s. He was an autodidact, an inventor, a craftsman, and an artist of a high order who specialized in woodworking, cabinetry, welding, stained glass, and furniture design.

After some pleasantries, Alan started to walk towards the Center's main entrance, with the Black Sheep group following behind him.

"So this is the Russell Center. It was, um, originally built as the Murray Body Company, and they made auto bodies for the, oh, for the Dodge Brothers, and Hupmobile, and Studebaker," Alan said, holding his right arm behind his back with his left hand as he walked. "This building has been in continuous production of one sort or another since it was built."

The asphalt parking lot was full of potholes and cracks, much like Detroit's streets. Alan wore a short-sleeve button-up and jeans, while our crew was more bundled up for the somewhat chilly morning.

"It was purchased in the sixties by Harry Helmsley of HelmsleySpear Properties," Alan continued with a pause for effect, "And then Leona sold it to pay her legal bills because, ya know," turning back to the group, "only little people pay taxes."

He chuckled, a sly cackle almost, waiting for others to respond, but everyone was still waking up. The reference to Leona Helmsley, that icon of cruelly selfish real-estate wealth and privilege, what we would surely call a white sheep, mostly passed over our heads.

Inside Alan's shop, which was some 20,000 square feet within the bowels of the Russell, were countless reminders of a previous era of craftsmanship. Alan had an assortment of Tiffany lamps, as well as a large collection of some two hundred lamps made by the John L. Gaumer Company, a 19th & 20th century manufacturer based out of Pittsburgh, many of them hanging from the ceilings throughout his shop. Alan found inspiration from the lamps because they were a fixture of the American Arts and Crafts period, the "heyday" of which occurred from 1900 to 1916. It had been all about reinventing society through design, and was very similar to the artistic renaissance that we aspired to catalyze.

Alan was a native Detroiter if there ever was one. "I went to Pershing High School," he shared, "So local *through and through.*"

No one else seemed to hear him.

"Pershing High School—I don't know if you ever heard about it—it was named after John J. Pershing of World War I, a general." Alan paused momentarily for effect, then quipped, "And it was such a tough school, the school newspaper had an *obituary column.*"

Alan waited a beat or two, read the sleepy confusion on a few faces, and added, "I'm just kidding," belting out another chuckle as he did so.

Alan was good like that: an artist and a jokester all at once, inner child and inner artist all on display. Perhaps humor was one of the only ways to stay sane through all the ups and downs in Detroit. I could never forget a few of the things he had said back in 2011. One was: "For years I've said, 'Just when you think Detroit can't get any worse, it does. And just when you think it's about to get better, *it doesn't!*'"

Another moment I remembered vividly was Alan's description of needing to reinvent himself after his traditional business, which included doing a lot of woodwork and cabinetry inside suburban Detroit homes, largely vanished after the Great Recession. It was at that point that Alan taught himself a new craft: making fine wood furniture. Alan saw the American Arts & Crafts movement as the beginning of modern furniture. Inspired, he taught himself how to design a chair by cutting a single piece of plywood into eighty or ninety pieces, minimizing waste. The chairs were beautiful, wonderfully designed, and comfortable. I knew this for a fact, having bought two of them on that first visit.

"You want to know my mission statement?" he asked us as we followed him around his shop, sensing his captive audience. Again, pausing for effect: "*Stay in business!*"

Finally sufficiently awake to keep up with Alan, we all laughed at that one. He was so memorable, and was such a great example of reinvention and renewal.

His furniture would go on to win prizes, and Alan taught himself how to sell what he made to ever more consumers, including through eBay. And, after he taught himself to be a master craftsman with furniture, he taught others. Alan taught both metal shop and woodworking classes at the College for Creative Studies in Detroit as well as a furniture design course at Wayne State University.

People like Alan gave me hope for America. He dedicated his life to his craft and, guided by a kind of ethical or moral compass, to others. He described leaving his previous "j-o-b" as a product developer at a stained-glass company years prior following an ethical disagreement with his boss. He ridiculed political corruption in ways that reminded me of Uncle Joe. And, at his core, Alan was an artist and a teacher above all else, and was dedicated to the mission of education.

The opposite of a money whore, Alan was unapologetic about turning his art into a means to keep a shop, keep doing what he loved, and help others. It was all for a purpose that worked from scarcity—the original wreck of the Russell Center—to a different kind of abundance, visible in artistic craft and renewal of place and people. This was the creative mindset, the opposite of politics. And it was why people like Alan and Uncle Joe gave me hope for America's moral salvation, because God knows that moral authority was not held in Washington, DC or in the halls of high finance. Worse, even in the colleges, universities, and non-profit cultural institutions, including most religious institutions, everyone was in bed with money for money's sake.

In fact, Alan and a legendary Detroit printmaker named Amos Kennedy were the first two artists to set up shop inside the Russell Industrial Center when a million square feet was opened up to artists. With around 150 tenants, it was billed as "home to the largest artist community in the Midwest." At one point, Alan realized that virtually every artist who took up shop in the Russell could be traced back to him or to Amos.

In the years that had passed since my first trip to Detroit and my introduction to Alan, his tone had changed a great deal. The reason was simple: Detroit had become a place of opportunity.

"You've got people that are coming to this city from all over the country and from all over the world because there's opportunity here," he exclaimed.

He talked about all the energy in Midtown. All the construction. All the entrepreneurs setting up shop. People were making money. Every week, something new appeared. Downtown was hopping too. New restaurants. New building projects. A couple of new hotels. Apparently even Eastpointe, formerly East Detroit, which bordered 8 Mile Road, a predominantly Black neighborhood, was showing signs of life. This was definitely a new Alan, shedding his preternatural cynicism for signs of renewal. It was also a new Detroit. The city still faced many challenges—deep traumas and haunting wounds—yet now there were also beacons of light shining. From the Russell, Alan pointed towards Midtown and Downtown, where a renaissance in fact was underway.

If Detroit could make a comeback, we started to imagine, any place in America could. Seeing those artists and entrepreneurs flock to Detroit like moths to a flame was inspiring. It wasn't just that they were drawn to opportunity; it was also that they were drawn to the like-minded, the like-circumstanced, the like-hopeful. There seemed to be something happening here that would become increasingly clear to us as we toured. Detroit was part of a broader pattern: when you visit the places in America where some of the most significant cultural renewal and reinvention has taken place over the past decade or two, whether that's New Orleans after Hurricane Katrina or former mill towns like Greenville, South Carolina, or Pittsburgh or Detroit, you will discover a common theme: the artists arrived first.

As the Black Sheep traveled around the country in the 2010s, urban and rural places that had been left for dead were becoming outposts of creativity, inspiring artists and tribes of entrepreneurs and social innovators to set up shop and get to work. Against the odds, in such places it became "all for one and one for all." In Detroit, they called it "Detroit Vs. Everybody," a term coined by the synonymous clothing brand. White, Black, and everyone in between were in it together. Individual success would depend on collective success. They started from a place of profound vulnerability, places bombed-out and riven by fault lines, and they built from there.

In these petri dishes of reinvention, growing communities of creatives become energy multipliers for everyone else, a symbol of optimism and resilience. "Go see what's happening over there," people will say, pointing to places where the artists and entrepreneurs congregate. These creative communities, bustling with energy, caused others to believe that change was possible, and importantly they operated completely beyond the radar of the media and political machines.

As we visited these businesses and social entrepreneurs, we were also able to see some of the fruits of our first co-conspiracy: Giving Tuesday.

"Yo, Pedah" intoned the deep, authoritative voice of Marlowe Stoudamire. "We still on for this afternoon?"

"Yes, sir!" I replied, "Just let me know where to meet you."

"Aite. Cool. So where are you now?"

"I'm here at Ponyride with Phil. He says hello."

"Ahh! The Fresh Prince!" Marlowe bellowed with a big laugh, "Give him my best!"

Looking back to Phil across the table from me, Marlowe's nickname immediately felt right. After all, in his early 20s Phil had been a male model in Europe, New York, and Tokyo—runways and magazine covers and everything—though that was "back in the day." He had since become one of the most important social entrepreneurs and community builders of his generation in Detroit.

Phil Cooley hadn't grown up in the Motor City like Marlowe had. He was from Marysville, Michigan, around two hours away, a small town of about 10,000 people in the "thumb" of the state. But by the time I was sitting across from him and talking with Marlowe on the phone, Phil had become a legend in Detroit, near the epicenter of a lot of the entrepreneurial energy that had helped the city come back from the dead.

"Marlowe calls you the Fresh Prince," I told Phil, muting my phone for a second.

We both laughed.

"Marlowe's awesome!" Phil enthused, as if talking about family.

Both Phil and Marlowe were inspired to be part of the Black Sheep, and we felt lucky and inspired to know them. We parked at Ponyride, on both bus tours, a 30,000 square-foot creative incubator for entrepreneurs, makers, artists, and more. People like Phil or Marlowe, or Nan Braun in Kokomo, Indiana, struck us as the real heroes in America. They were re-inventing their communities from the bottom up with artistry and entrepreneurship, characteristic of a generation rising up throughout America whom we encountered on our bus tours.

I had known Phil longer than Marlowe, when Phil was known to be near the center of Detroit's newfound entrepreneurial energy. Back then, his big venture was Slows BBQ, a restaurant just off Michigan Avenue in Downtown. Slows BBQ became renowned for its slow-cooked meats and original BBQ sauce.

But the business was also a hub for Phil's real passion: building a community of social changemakers.

For Phil, being in Detroit was always a choice. After returning to the United States as a twenty-four-year-old fresh from Europe after his modeling days, he picked Detroit not because he was a Michigan native, but because he was drawn to its deep diversity, its grit, and the daunting challenges the city faced. Phil was an artist, and like the other artists drawn to the Russell Industrial Center, he was drawn to the notion that the only way Detroit was going to come back from the dead following the 1980s crack epidemic was if a community formed there that crossed all races and walks of life, a community that could act as what he called "a stone soup."

"Sixteen years ago, when I moved here it was, you know . . ." he paused as he tried to describe the city as it had looked to him at the time. "It was that 'stone soup' thing where everyone had one ingredient and, therefore, we were able to make something special."

The old story of stone soup made sense. A destitute, penniless woman is found adding stones to water and is asked, "What are you making?" "Stone soup," she says. "And it will be better if we could add some salt." One person finds salt. "And some potatoes." Another person finds potatoes. "And carrots, turnips, perhaps a bit of chicken." And strangers each pitch in with something, one thing each, and at the end of it all, there was delicious soup for everyone.

Phil loved that Detroit, circa the 1990s, a time for pioneering, akin to the Wild West. Back then it was truly Detroit versus everybody. Detroit was a place where even an ex-runway model in his twenties like Phil could have a voice and a role in finding solutions, could become one of the necessary ingredients for reinvention, and in the process its people could build a city in which to belong.

"It taught me to give others a voice as well, when I was eventually in a position to do so," he continued as we sat in Ponyride. "I was able to realize that it's never just me. It's about all of us together."

Marlowe Stoudamire was one of those people in the stone soup of Detroit whom Phil loved: a key community leader from East Detroit who had the type of presence that magnetized most everyone. His essence and booming personality and voice made him akin to Muhammad Ali, one of his childhood heroes. In honor of the fact, we nicknamed him the "Ali" of the Black Sheep. His powerful energy dominated rooms and stages; his expansive presence was matched by a powerful baritone voice.

"Let's jump right into it," Marlowe began his remarks at the Detroit Policy Conference a couple months before with characteristic "real talk." "Now everybody loves Detroit. Seriously: everybody loves us now. But at the end of the day, it's always been Detroit versus everybody. If it's gonna really happen, we have to be against everyone and for each other, and we have to stick together."

Marlowe had a way of speaking up for everyone, including the unheard. The unseen. Those on the East Side of Detroit who were voiceless. Powerless. People left behind by the "new Detroit" story in *The New York Times*. People for whom the opportunities in Midtown and Downtown continued to seem like a distant mirage. They still lived in the ruined and desolate pockets of the city, places where the public-education system was still in tatters. Hell, just five years earlier Detroit filed for Chapter 9—the largest municipal bankruptcy ever in the United States. And like America itself, Detroit was by no means out of the depths of darkness, pain, hopelessness, and despair brought on by globalization, the crack epidemic, and the Great Recession.

"A lot of people in the community are still having trouble believing the so-called 'comeback story' that we're talking about," he explained to the audience of mostly business people gathered for the conference. "Well, it's not because they're angry. It's not because they're jealous. They don't have an issue with you. It's because for a great deal of them, that comeback really isn't happening."

Despite his keen-eyed understanding of Detroit's realities, Marlowe had a deep faith and optimism that things could be better, and would keep getting better. He was an entrepreneur as much as an activist. His currency was people and relationships, and it seemed like everyone knew him. Joining forces with people like Phil excited Marlowe, even if this also entailed a little healthy competition. With the same hunger I saw in London, people in Detroit like Phil and Marlowe sought to be first to land a deal, though for them the deal was about renewal, purpose, and creating abundance out of scarcity.

※

Detroit is an expansive city, just over 142 square miles, yet Phil was happy to give me a ride wherever I needed to go to meet Marlowe. We savored the drive as a chance to catch up on life, especially talking about our daughters, who were roughly the same age. By then, Phil had become successful enough as an entrepreneur that he could invest in others' businesses. His wife Kate, a primary co-pilot leading Ponyride and in life, always seemed to keep Phil on track. She was a force: a leader, a great mom, and all that complemented Phil. They seemed like the dream team if you wanted to get something done.

"Look for the giant cow's head," Marlowe had texted, along with a cross-street, off Mack Avenue and Lennox.

"Cool," I replied. "Phil's giving me a ride and wants to say hello."

"Ahhh!" Marlowe came back quickly.

As much as Marlowe liked and respected Phil, and would willingly partner with him on projects, he also played things real coy when we showed up at the meeting spot. Marlowe didn't want Phil to steal his deal—not this one. The thought would never enter Phil's head, but Marlowe was animated. He had a big vision for restoring and reinventing an old Detroit landmark, originally erected by Ira Wilson and Sons Dairy as a beacon for ice cream in the 1960s. Now it was just called the Giant Cow Head, which looked abandoned yet appeared in Eminem's *8 Mile* and had become somewhat famous after that. The building had been for sale for about $80,000, and Marlowe had a vision for turning it into something special.

When Phil and I arrived, Marlowe's eyes darted around a bit, as if he wanted to save the rest of the story for our one-on-one time. I hadn't quite realized it, but Marlowe wanted to pitch me on the idea, which was just getting some momentum. And here I was showing up with the Fresh Prince of Detroit.

As we got out of the car, Marlowe greeted Phil with a fist clasp and a hug. "What up, Fresh Prince?" he said with a big grin and laugh, yet behind it all was a sense of reserve.

Phil laughed too, relaxed and chill, wearing his BLK SHP hat proudly. "Wait—are you working on a project with the Cow Head?"

Marlowe found all the right words to create a smoke-screen. He hadn't lined up investors yet and wasn't ready to potentially bring in the Fresh Prince, even though Phil might be a perfect partner. In that particular moment, though—such early days of the idea—Marlowe didn't want his vision to get scooped. As I came to understand after Phil left, Marlowe's ideas were expansive beyond just the Giant Cow Head. Once it was just us two, Marlowe filled me in on his vision for the next five to ten years, his piece of the stone soup for Detroit's reinvention. He wanted to affect a whole group of blocks in the area and create a community center to boot.

That came later. What happened that afternoon was different. As I watched Phil and Marlowe gab and laugh, I was struck by how much I admired these two entrepreneurs and the way they lived their lives. While each was motivated to create things that could be lucrative, money wasn't their primary life goal. They could be competitors on projects or deals, but more than that they were brothers from other mothers. They bled for Detroit and for their community. It was such a far cry from the culture on the West Coast and Silicon Valley. I saw one of the first prototypes for what became Uber, then watched for years as its founding CEO, Travis Kalanick, acted like a giant asshole to everyone. Kalanick didn't seem to give a shit about the community, Uber's drivers, his girlfriend's friends, or anyone but himself. And it showed.

If America was going to have a renaissance and reinvent from the bottom up, it wasn't going to be thanks to the next Uber or

Silicon Valley startup. What America needed wasn't more Silicon Valley arrogance or Wall Street money whores; it needed more of the generosity and compassion that we saw with Giving Tuesday. It needed more people like Phil and Kate Cooley and Marlowe Stoudamire. Detroit's stone soup was merely a microcosm for America's renewal.

In fact, "stone soup" was not a bad way to describe and harness that creative renaissance. All the country needed was time, and enough Black Sheep to come out of the fold and make it to the time and place when and where they could add their contribution.

That revolution would have to be improvised.

CHAPTER THIRTEEN

RESETTING THE LINEAGE

I was more than half-asleep on the couch in the Dutch Flat house's living room when my phone vibrated on the wood floor. It was odd to have a call come through, since I distinctly recalled putting the phone on Airplane Mode, yet there it was, rattling on the floor. Picking up the phone and squinting with one eye, I saw that it was Linda, which caused me to sit up quickly. During the week, she usually called only when there was a problem.

"Peter . . ." she said in a composed, yet emotional tone.

I knew immediately, having expected a call like this for years.

"Your father just passed . . ." She could barely get the words out, then burst out crying.

There was a lot of noise in the background too: voices, cars, and commotion.

"It's okay, Linda." I said. "It's . . ." I was at a loss.

During the immunotherapy treatment that was prescribed after Dad was diagnosed with melanoma, the doctors also diagnosed him with a rare degenerative disease that left him largely paralyzed, confined to a wheelchair, for the last couple years. Linda took care of him the whole time. They made the decision to leave California and lived in a charming little house on the big island of Hawaii with a view overlooking the vast Pacific Ocean. Dad wasn't in pain and always kept in good spirits, but he was no longer able to speak or even type. His extremely limited ability to communicate was the hardest part for him because his mind remained sound.

On the phone, poor Linda could barely talk. I picked up enough details to understand that she was in a Costco parking lot and she needed me to talk with the police and paramedics on the scene.

"Hello, Peter?" a man's voice pointedly asked.

"Yes, sir."

"This is Officer Mike Anderson of the Kona Police," he said, speaking quickly. "We've been doing chest compressions on your dad for about fifteen minutes. We can keep going but . . ." He lost some of his officious, authoritative voice. "I think . . . he's gone."

"It's okay, sir," I replied, now focused on imagining the scene. "I understand. We understand."

"I'm so sorry," he continued. "Your step-mom is very emotional. You may want to come down here."

"I'm in California."

Pause. "Okay, I'm going to put her back on."

"Thank you."

I walked slowly around the living room of the old house as I held the phone to my ear. It was the same house where six and a half years earlier Linda had panicked and called 9-1-1. This time, she was calling *me* for help. I was in a mild state of shock, the long-expected news and the many old memories flooding my mind. But, hearing her voice, I was keenly aware that what I was experiencing was not as shocking as what Linda was going through there in the Costco parking lot, surrounded by paramedics and police as Dad passed on. Most of my attention in that moment was focused on being there for Linda, but I also paused to honor that Dad was passing on right then in those dramatic seconds, the two of us separated by the Pacific Ocean. Just where his soul went, I didn't know, but I was sure it would be better than the state he had been in for the past several years.

I wasn't afraid of death, so much as curious about what might be on the other side.

Linda cried profusely on the other end of the line. She sounded both profoundly alone and not. I could hear lots of voices and beeps and chatter over the emergency personnel radio. I closed my eyes, trying to visualize the scene. Linda had bought a handicapped-accessible car and had it shipped to Hawaii from the States. That day had been their first trip out in about nine months, since COVID hit.

"Your dad was eating a hot dog from Costco, and he choked," she said, sobbing uncontrollably.

In the background, radios beeped. Vehicles idled. And doors slammed—perhaps the back doors of an ambulance, I wondered.

"It's okay, Linda," I said. "It's okay," I kept repeating calmly. "It's all going to be okay. Right now, it's important for you to just sit down and breathe."

"Okay," she said, sounding more calm.

Dad had been agnostic, never able to understand why, if there was a God, bad things happened to good people. As much as I tried to persuade him otherwise, he didn't believe much in an afterlife, so he had fought tooth-and-nail for each day, and had been resilient and optimistic. I was sure that had been the spirit of his outing to Costco.

"He had a very good life, and you had both suffered enough," I continued.

"I know," she said, slipping words in between the occasional gasps, "but I wasn't ready . . . to let him go . . . *today*."

"I know, Linda, I know. I'm so sorry. It's all going to be okay," was my mantra. "It's going to be okay."

I felt numb, but summoned the energy to just be there, to send Linda calm energy and love. She seemed to settle down more and more. It was hard to imagine her state of shock, but she was a strong person and resilient herself. For all of my misgivings, she had stayed by my dad's side through thick and thin.

After calling my brother to let him know the news, I tried reaching Mom, but she wasn't home. As I looked out onto Dutch Flat through the large living room windows, I noticed that a warm light was starting to kiss the pines. It was approaching the "magic hour" just before sunset, Dad's favorite time of day.

Walking down the hallway, I stopped to appreciate the pictures of Dad hung on the wall. One of him in Grandpa's lap when he was a toddler, another of him and Grandpa holding me as a newborn, and a handful of pictures from his boyhood at the end of the hall. There was just one photo of his whole family: Dad with Aunt Liz and Grandma and Grandpa, and my other aunt and uncle, who had passed away years before. Aunt Liz was now the last sibling alive. ("I'm the black sheep of the family," she would say later that night, as if she had thought a lot about that.)

Emotion filled my chest as I turned into the master bedroom. I opened the door to the closet and found a large box labeled, in what I assumed was my grandmother's handwriting, "Richard's papers + scrapbooks." I pulled the box down and onto the bed. My grandmother had been known to save everything. I had found the box earlier that year, and I returned to it now, knowing it contained items that would help me understand Dad's essence in new ways.

Removing the lid, I entered a time capsule of his youth. A Ziploc bag contained his Boy Scouts of America membership card and seemingly all his childhood birthday cards. Still deeper, his first Red Cross membership card was on top of an *In Numberland* workbook. Thumbing through the worksheets, which were graded, Dad received a grade of 100% on most every one of them, already saved by his mother.

What interested me most, however, was deeper into the box. Beneath the newspaper clippings and workbooks, beneath the commencement program for his high school, and beneath the accolades were six pieces of art. Paintings and drawings. They were remarkably detailed and well-crafted paintings and drawings. One gorgeous acrylic depicted a Native American dance ceremony. Another showed a finely-crafted blue dragon in inks. Another was a watercolor of nature. And, finally, a magnificent tiger lily-like flower, intricately crafted and detailed. Each read "Rick Sims, Art 2, Period 4, Locker 11" at the bottom.

I stood with the works laid out on the bed, marveling.

Like so many, Dad had been a talented artist, yet his life's influences pushed him away from that part of himself. He had been a Black Sheep at heart. And like many Black Sheep, he hadn't always been able to fully express himself. One of his great aspirations was that his sons could do things differently, that they would find their fullest expressions in life. He wanted us to have a mother with deep emotional intelligence and creativity. I had a keen appreciation for why; Dad's identity and voice were never fully his own.

You see, Dad was named Richard M. Sims III, and always felt like he was in his father's shadow. His father, my grandfather, Richard Sims Jr., whom we called Grandpa Judge, was highly respected: the former District Attorney of Marin County and a state appeals court judge. Bobby Kennedy and Cesar Chavez met in his living room. So, yeah, those were big shoes to fill, and in fact, all three Richard M. Simses had been lawyers. Dad, meanwhile, told me every chance he got that being a lawyer "sucked," and that all the lawyers he knew were unhappy. So for all those reasons, and maybe more, Dad wanted his kids to be able to break the cycle and have their own identities and paths in life. Mom firmly agreed, especially since her brother had been Frank E. Carroll III and always resented it too. So Mom and Dad came from pioneering California families led by strong patriarchies and determined to break "the pressure of the patriarchy" with their own kids.

And so, in their wisdom, my parents decided to give their kids their own, truly original names, including middle names after animals. Sitting in the sunroom of their run-down Victorian apartment on Sacramento Street a few months before I was born, they talked about a boy's name. They both loved the name "Peter," since they both liked the "Peters" they knew, and Mom's mom had a dog she loved named "Peter." As for a middle name, the country was about to celebrate America's bicentennial month and year in July 1976, the same month they were expecting their first child. "Eagle" was a logical choice for patriotic reasons, and also because the eagle was the most sacred and revered bird in many native American traditions and totems. The eagle totem, which my parents also discussed that day, represented being able to live in the spirit realm balanced with Mother Earth.

So that day they decided that if the newborn was a boy, the baby's name would be Peter Eagle Sims.

Break the fucking patriarchy. Create a new lineage.

After placing the contents back in the box and replacing the lid, I choked up. I needed some fresh air. Walking out onto the front porch, I wondered if Dad's spirit was there, around one of the chairs on the porch where he so often smoked a pipe during the "magic hour" as he just stared off into the trees. Dutch Flat was where his soul belonged: a town forgotten by time, enveloped by nature, where everyone waved.

As I walked down the hill into town, wisps of fog lifted up towards the mountain ridge in the distance, maybe a half a mile away. Another plume of white smoke lifted from one of the houses in town—I couldn't tell which one—against the backdrop of golden light. This is where Dad had had some of his fondest memories.

I walked down the main street past the old, white, dilapidating United Methodist Church and remembered all the annual Fourth of July parades that Dad announced from its top steps, a job he'd loved for twenty-five years straight. The soft light lit up all the Ponderosa pines behind the church, maybe ten or fifteen of them, just glowing.

I imagined Dad at the top of the church steps, behind the mic in his red and white outfit, his Dutch Flat hat atop his head. This town was where his soul belonged.

Turning off the main street to walk up the hill towards Grandma's old house, I passed a woman walking two dogs. She was momentarily startled, then warm and friendly like everyone in that small town. She started talking with a neighbor farther up on the hill, another of the roughly 200 residents. People really cared about each other in Dutch Flat, Dad had told us, and he wanted us and our kids to experience that. That was something big-city folk often forgot in their atomized worlds. Here in Dutch Flat, with all its appearance of vulnerability—the older wooden structures in need of paint and care, the older residents—there was in fact the tensile strength of community greater than you might find on a single big-city block.

By the time I reached Grandma Dale's old house, it was nearly twilight. The trees were all now enveloped by nature, while the fading daylight graced the clouds. Smoke emerged from a stovepipe towards the back of the house, lit by the family that now resided in it, and I imagined Dad's memories there— in praise of the shadows and the light. The days of his carefree youth: a boy running barefoot around the backyard, into town, up the street to the community pool, in Fourth of July parades long before anyone thought he was supposed to officiate them. Also the nights when Grandma became drunk and enraged and threw pots and pans around, like the night she kicked Aunt Liz out of the house. The years during which Grandma's addiction nearly destroyed her and the family.

A tear streamed down my cheek for that innocent and sweet boy, that artist at heart, whose mother always wanted him to be something else. Perhaps President of the United States. I shuddered to imagine her own prison. It was a moment for love and compassion for all. Dad ultimately did life his way, and gave my brother and me our own identities and our own leases on life, which had allowed me to break the lineage.

Someone once shared a thought that summed up the quest: "Most black sheep of their family become self-healers, break their generational curses, fear, guilt, and shame, and start their own lineage."

Here, in a sentence, was why a human being trying to just be human can be such hard, hard work. Alcoholism and mental health issues may have been a source of shame for my grandmother and Dad, yet he and Mom had given me the permission (and the tools) to start a new lineage. When my daughter was born, I vowed that she would be unburdened by those past traumas.

Before night fell, I started to walk back down the hill and into the small downtown with the old historic Dutch Flat Hotel, post office, and general store. I put in my earpieces and pressed play. *One Tree Hill* by U2 came on. It was the perfect song for the moment: a song Bono wrote in memory of one of his beloved roadies, Greg Carroll, who had died in a motorcycle accident. It was said that Bono recorded the vocals in one take, unable to do so again. Bono was apparently so emotional about the loss of his good friend that for years he didn't want to sing the song publicly. As I walked into the sunset, the soulful, beautiful song mixed a soft benediction with a celebration of life.

A couple of months later, snow was on the ground in Dutch Flat. It was January, and pine trees everywhere were set off by white. The "mountain house," as my daughter Riley called it, became a cozy lodge during winter, complete with a large stone fireplace in the living room. Leather couches and chairs formed a U-shape around the hearth, each draped with Pendleton wool blankets, patterned with multi-colored geometric shapes. The walls were covered with art, from paintings of pastures and mountainscapes to Ansel Adams photos of Yosemite to a hanging Navajo blanket. Since Dad's passing, I understood all of them as reminders of his sensitivity and artistry. With the snow, Uncle Joe had a few days off work. He called. We made plans for him to come over one afternoon, just to hang out.

Around 2 p.m. or so he limped through the front door into the living room, wearing his well-worn, first-edition Black Sheep hat. After a brief embrace, I asked if he wanted a beer.

A two-second pause, then "Sure!"

He plopped down on one of the couches as a fire roared. I had installed a surround-sound system in the living room earlier in the year and had a "mellow rock" playlist going.

"This is my kinda music," he mused as I came back holding a Coors Light, retrieved from a cooler on the side porch. The can was a bit corroded from sitting in the cooler since summer, but as he popped the top Uncle Joe didn't seem to give a damn.

"Oh, this?" I replied, turning my ear as *Danny's Song*, an often-forgotten early Kenny Loggins and Jim Messina folk ditty, played.

The snow on the ground, the quiet, the warmth of the fire— it was a good afternoon to just chill, and since it was after 1 p.m., I was done working. It had been nearly four years since I stopped taking work meetings or calls after 1 p.m., the beginning of the happiest work years of my life. Afternoons were for friends, movies, curiosity, play, relaxation, creativity, and chilling—just like that afternoon. And sitting there listening to *Danny's Song*, I could tell that, while Uncle Joe was the hardest working person I knew growing up, he was more than ready for retirement and chilling.

If only Aunt Liz would let him! We laughed about that one. She kept track of their finances, and they weren't able to retire just yet, but he had just finished paying off his truck, and was in talks to sell it, so the light was at the end of the tunnel. With that light also came a sense of what was to come, after the long and weary roads and loads, with the soundtrack of his life playing in the background.

As I sat across from him in a reclining chair, our conversation turned to music.

"Your favorite song is *Sympathy for the Devil*, right?"

"Mmm. Yeah; I'd say so . . ." he replied, pausing as he listened.

"So Bob Seger is a close second?"

"Bob Seger is probably my favorite musician, just overall."

"Not the Stones?"

"I love the Stones," he said, looking into the fire, "but Bob Seger is my favorite."

Flipping through playlists, I pulled up Bob Seger's top tracks, then pushed Play. *Old Time Rock & Roll* came up first. It's the type of song that made you just want to get up and dance: *that kind of music that just soothes the soul . . . with that old time rock 'n' roll.* Yeah—that seemed like Uncle Joe's music. I pictured him barreling through the mountain roads and passes, tapping his steering wheel with his thumbs to classic American rock-and-roll songs like this. Best corner office in the world, with a corresponding soundtrack.

But I also knew—had long known—that there was much more to Uncle Joe than that: a melancholy in his soul beneath the stoicism and dirt that usually only a few beers and music would reveal.

I saw it in his eyes soon after the next song, *Against the Wind*, came on: *it seems like yesterday; but it was long ago.* It was as if Uncle Joe suddenly went into a trance, holding his beer on his right leg as his dark-blue eyes panned to the right, staring off outside, sinking into the couch. The fingers of his free hand tapped the arm rest, perhaps a muscle memory. He seemed lost in the moment.

"What are you thinking?" I asked as the song was coming to an end, curious about the narrative behind his sullen eyes. Was it nostalgia or regret, or maybe just memories?

"Oh, I dunno," he replied, gently glancing at me, still in a trance-like state.

"Does the song bring back memories?"

"Memories? Nah. I just like Bob Seger."

"His music seems to look back a lot. Into the past."

"Yeah. I love that about his music."

"So you like to live in the past?" I prodded with a smile, which of course he did, routinely thinking back to those glory days of his youth, as so many do.

"Times that were *simpler!*" he replied in a sharper tone, perhaps foreshadowing that he was about to tweak me with his wit.

"So I'm the one here responsible for holding to an optimistic vision about the future, while you're the one who looks in the rearview mirror?" I continued with a chuckle.

"Ack!" he blurted, as if he wanted to come over and smack his nephew or something, if only he had more energy.

After a thoughtful pause, he held up his hands and articulated, "I'm a *guarded* pessimist."

That was Uncle Joe all right. It all made sense, the better you got to know him.

"You know, I've worked for over fifty years," he went on. "Well, full-time at least. I started working in the woods with my dad when I was *thirteen.*"

"Man, that's wild. You've earned days like this." And then a thought as another song queued up on the playlist. "I feel like your inner artist is a musician."

That brought a smile, as he hoisted himself up off the couch and limped over towards me to sit on the old wooden and embroidered bench in front of the fireplace, just to my left. He wanted me to hear what came next.

"It is," he said plaintively. "I wish I hadn't stopped playing the piano."

"How long did you play?" I asked, knowing that he had played piano in his youth, yet never having heard the full story.

"Oh . . . well, from when I was five until I was about ten."

"That's a while." And as I said it, I did the mental math. And three years after he stopped playing the piano, he started working in the woods with his dad.

"And I was good, too. I may have been able to play in a band like this," he said, pointing up to the music.

"Why'd you stop?"

"Oh, I got to that age where it wasn't cool to practice, you know," he said with a grimace, as if he was judging himself or felt regret.

"I get that," I responded. Who among us hasn't let our decisions be made by what we think others decide is cool, uncool? "At least your love of music never ceased."

Now that Uncle Joe was 73, he needed to just retire and listen to music. Bob Seger took him to a place that was the real him. He would tell me later that for years after Jennie's death, he couldn't listen to his favorite Seger song, *Like A Rock*. It reminded him too much of her. And for a while there he couldn't listen to *any* Bob Seger song, for that matter. But that snowy day in January we just sat there for a while, listening and laughing, connecting during a special day together, a day almost as special as those we spent in his truck.

After maybe ten Seger songs, it was time for a change, so I told him I was going to play some music for him that was meaningful to me, and put on Pearl Jam's *Ten*. It was my coming-of-age album from high school. *Ten* was quite the contrast with Bob Seger, full of energy and optimism and enthusiasm, punctuated by the album's landmark song, *Alive*.

It wasn't the Stones or Bob Seger or one of those countless southern bands Uncle Joe had an affinity for—from Lynyrd Skynyrd to Alabama to the Marshall Tucker Band. But he seemed to like Pearl Jam. Still deep in thought, he stared across the room, still with a hint of melancholy, before standing up and going outside to grab another beer. Kicking back in my reclining chair, I thumbed through playlists, pondering the next move.

"Ugh!" he bellowed as he walked back in, holding a Coors Light can even more corroded the previous one, "You *gotta* clean out that cooler!"

True, but it didn't prevent him from popping open another can and taking a sip as I put on a Rolling Stones song and tried to change the subject. I told him how I had been listening recently to a podcast with Paul McCartney, who was saying how much Elvis had influenced him and the Beatles.

"Elvis?"

"Yeah, Elvis. Did you ever get into his music?"

"Not really," he said, as he took a big sip of beer, "but there was that one song of his . . . what was it? Oh, yeah: *In the Ghetto*."

"*In the Ghetto*?"

"Yeah. I think that's it."

That was news to me, but when I searched for the song, sure enough, there it was: *In the Ghetto* by Elvis Presley. After clicking Play, it was immediately clear this was a very different song than any other Elvis song I had heard. Singing in a sympathetic voice, Elvis told the story of a poor baby being born in the inner city.

Once again, Uncle Joe stared off into the distance as the song played, holding his beer on his right knee, deep in thought with those sad eyes. I prodded again, but all he could murmur was, "Those kids . . ." It took me right back to Nick and that night with Harold and the boys, and the spirit of love and recovery. In that moment, well beneath the stoicism, I felt like I could feel his full heart and empathy, his humanity.

Uncle Joe, transported to some place listening to those words, looked as if he was about to shed a tear. It came to an end and then there was silence but for the slight crackle of the fire, silence that must have lasted two minutes. I followed my own thoughts. I guessed that after a drink or two most loving parents think about their kids. Uncle Joe was no different, especially as the music played and opened up such a contemplative mood. I can't remember exactly how we got onto it, but it seemed the most natural thing. We started talking about Nick.

"I remember the day it hit me," Uncle Joe said, and then described an experience he had visiting the addiction recovery center around the holidays.

"They put on a play about some scenes out of the Bible, and in one scene Nick was playing Jesus. The curtain came up and he was on a cross."

"Wow."

"Yeah. That's when it *really* hit me," he said, speaking slowly, searching for the right words. "It wasn't abstract no more."

"Nick looked like Jesus?"

"Yeah. He looked just like Jesus. But not just that; it was also my own son up on the cross," he went on. "And it helped me feel closer to God."

"Wow. That sounds like a powerful moment."

"It was."

"I remember how we talked about how the church helped you find self-acceptance back around then."

"Self-acceptance?" He pondered that a bit, then said, "Well, with God's love, it helped me find *self-forgiveness*."

"Ahhh," I replied, understanding coming over me. I remembered how hard it had been for Uncle Joe to forgive himself for Jennie's death. He had carried that weight around his neck for years.

"I didn't even know about self-forgiveness. That's not how I was raised. We were . . ." he sought the word, "very pragmatic."

By forgiving rather than judging himself, he was accepting his full humanity, as I saw it.

"That's powerful," I said. "Self-acceptance is one of the hardest things to find. Once you get there, you're truly free."

"Yeah. It took me damn near my whole life to get there, but when I finally did, I could finally . . . *relax* a bit."

I felt similar, especially after accepting my mental health diagnosis fully so long ago. Although I never felt defined by it, now six or seven years after the hospitalization, I knew I was one of the lucky ones. As my doctor said, it was a mild case. If anything, I felt like my wiring became an incredible creative asset. By that I mean that my "nut" mind allowed me to see the world and its patterns differently than others, to envision new ways of working and building companies, organizations, and institutions.

Just as our greatest strengths have corresponding weaknesses, our greatest potential vulnerabilities can end up as superpowers masquerading as weaknesses.

After that, we talked about my dad a bit, and about how he had left detailed instructions for his memorial service, down to the songs he wanted to be played there. As we stood there, looking out the window out onto the sea of green trees, Uncle Joe looked pensive again.

Then he surprised me. "I don't think many people would come to my memorial service."

"You've got a lot of fans, Uncle Joe!" I wouldn't let him get away with that.

"Anyhow . . . the only thing I'd request is one song."

"Which song is that?"

"Well, it's *The Ballad of Easy Rider* by the Byrds," he said, glancing at me. "You know; from the movie *Easy Rider.*"

The reference was a bit before my time, but I at least knew of the movie, and summoned vague pictures of bikers.

"With Peter Fonda and . . ." Uncle Joe looked down, trying to remember.

"Right, and . . . and . . . Dennis Hopper!"

"*That's it!*" he replied while pointing upwards, sounding impressed, knowing his old age sometimes caused him to forget a name here and there.

Anyhow, *The Ballad of Easy Rider* was a song I wasn't familiar with, but I wasn't going to play it, not that day. I reminded him, "You're not going anywhere for a while, and we're counting on you to get out on the road with us on the next Black Sheep bus tour."

He laughed, wiping his chin with his hand, still gazing outside.

"No; I'm done!" he exclaimed. "It's up to your generation now. *I'm counting on the Black Sheep!*"

CHAPTER FOURTEEN

THE VITRUVIAN CHILD

The night before my daughter Riley's seventh birthday, Ed Catmull came over for dinner. It was happenstance, a fortuitous aligning of the stars. A couple other friends were joining us too, and so I set about preparing for a simple dinner at my house at the base of the Oakland Hills, full of art from the artists Black Sheep had supported through the years.

Two of Alan Kaniarz's elegantly designed wooden chairs, made from sustainably grown and harvested plywood, stood in the living room, a reminder of his reinvention, as well as Detroit's. A couple of Amos Kennedy's framed prints hung around the house, including one that read "NO EXTREME DANCING ALLOWED!" at the base of the staircase leading to the second floor. In the dining area just off the kitchen, one of Danny McGinnist Jr.'s paintings hung, inspired by the nature and plants around Mom's houseboat.

More than five years had passed since Ed and Riley first met outside Ed's house on Pacific Street in San Francisco, when Riley had been about eighteen months old. After asking me if he could hold her, Ed lifted my small, giggling daughter up over his head and exclaimed, "We made a movie about you, Riley!" He was referring to *InsideOut*, the film Pixar released in 2015, its lead character a little girl named Riley who wrestled with strong, conflicting emotions surrounding parents, an unwelcome move, and her own growing up. It was released the same year Riley Sims was born. Both Rileys were also blessed with significant reservoirs of joy, which help with all of life's traumas, a core theme of the movie.

Naturally, Riley had no memory of the original meeting, but she had many memories of Pixar movies and magic, and she had grown up with occasional visits with Ed. So when he showed up at the front door, she easily recognized him.

With the same enthusiasm he'd shown all those years earlier, Ed called out, "Hi, Riley!" This meeting of like minds happened just beyond my eyesight, my attention fully engaged in the kitchen, but I listened as Riley led him into the living room, doing a few cartwheels as she went.

"Those are some great cartwheels, Riley!" Ed remarked with an impish grin.

Ed was dressed in his usual blue jeans and a t-shirt, this one with an image from the Pixar short film *Bao*, about a Chinese mother whose sadness about her child moving out of her house eases when a dumpling she makes springs to life. I emerged from the kitchen to share a hug. We had about forty-five minutes before another two guests arrived.

I was behind on my prep as Ed walked into the kitchen. I

suggested that he sit down on one of the two wooden stools pulled up to the kitchen counter. He chose the one covered with about a dozen Hello Kitty stickers, a tell that it was Riley's. As we drank seltzer, and I puttered around the counters and the stove, Ed started to go down another rabbit hole, talking about the virtues of tonic water, somehow triggered by drinking seltzer water. This unscripted conversation, with Ed just in a flow, seemed like the perfect opportunity to show him something fun that I had ordered.

The Black Sheep had re-nicknamed Ed as "DaVinci." After all, even around Pixar, every time someone called Ed "The Pope," he felt like he had to add that he wasn't even Catholic and he had much more in common with the iconic renaissance man anyhow. Like Leonardo DaVinci, Ed was at his core a scientist whose inventions, beginning with a small, computer-animated 3D hand that he produced in graduate school, followed by collaborating with countless people at Pixar to invent an industry, ultimately earned him a Turing Award, considered the Nobel Prize for computer science. Additionally, I often ribbed Ed that his handwriting was worse than DaVinci's, who famously wrote backwards, from right to left, so that his words were legible only when viewed in a mirror. And Ed and DaVinci were also both notorious procrastinators: DaVinci left most of his works unfinished, while Ed spent two years just organizing his notes in order to produce a revised version of his book *Creativity, Inc.*

"With enough patience, I learn to wait even longer than DaVinci," he emailed one day, adding in his trademark deadpan humor, "It is good to have high aspirations."

The nickname DaVinci just felt right and Ed preferred it, so DaVinci he became.

Which is why, as a joke, I bought a 30-by-20-inch replica of DaVinci's famous Vitruvian Man on canvas. Ed, perched atop his Hello Kitty stool, grinned as I placed it on the counter in front of him.

"Ahhh," he commented, then paused, as if searching for words that matched the moment and realizing none were needed.

"Hey, Riley!" I called into the living room.

"Yeah?" she replied, plodding one foot after the other into the kitchen.

"You wanna paint with Ed?"

"Sure!" she chirped, and promptly ran over to open the drawers beneath a small table on the side of the kitchen, from which she retrieved a set of washable paints. Pulling the other wooden stool over near Ed, Riley plopped down next to him, looking over the canvas on the counter.

"Dad, can I have a paintbrush?" she asked, looking behind the sink at a bowl and jar that contained brushes, large and small.

I grabbed a few—one large brush and a couple of small ones—and Riley went to work. Ed seemed charmed and noticeably impressed by Riley's quick brush circles on the canvas, her focus, her confidence. As she hunched over DaVinci's Vitruvian Man, rapidly making it her own, he and I continued our conversation, mostly talking about Google, where for the past several years he and I had worked as advisors at the company's semi-secret innovation lab.

In her own world, Riley wasted no time, using a rich color palette of pink, purple, turquoise, orange, brown, and red to give her Vitruvian Man a whole new identity.

"Wow, Riley!" Ed commented after looking down at the nearly halfway completed work. "That's looking great."

He then picked up the larger brush, dipped it in turquoise paint, and started on the right side of the canvas, under the man's arm. Ed was understudy to Riley, who didn't miss a beat or stop her own brushstrokes. What struck me wasn't that Ed Catmull and my seven-year-old daughter were enhancing DaVinci's image with vivid colors, but that neither Riley nor Ed seemed to think about it. A child and an inner child, an artist and an inner artist, both at work together.

As Riley put the finishing touches on the painting, Ed and I stepped into the den, where he paused before the original Frank Gehry sketch of his personal journey to becoming a Black Sheep. As best I could, I recounted Gehry's explanation of each of its features, why the school, why the helicopter, just as Gehry had explained it to me ten years earlier. Ed nodded, his eyes on the image. I remarked how interesting it was that Gehry had been in his late forties before he really found his distinctive architectural and artistic voice. I explained how Gehry had used all those experiments on his house in Santa Monica to inform and inspire his designs for Disney Concert Hall in Los Angeles and the Guggenheim Bilbao.

"That's interesting," Ed replied, a phrase he used often and genuinely.

"And, you know," I continued, "Gehry said the same thing you've said—that in life there really is no mountaintop."

"There's no mountaintop!" Ed quickly rejoined, looking me straight in the eye. "You're *never* there."

This was a conversation he and I had many times before.

"The journey really is the reward," I said as Ed smiled and nodded. In my kitchen Riley was improving DaVinci. Ed Catmull was in my den, gaining insight and feelings of kinship from a sketch by Frank Gehry. The ghost of our fathers, the presence of Uncle Joe's picture across the room, and Mom's encouragement that the sky would be the limit in life was also present. It was one of the most connected moments I have ever had with Ed: a moment when a truth was being conveyed that was profound and powerful, something that needed to be internalized.

That really is the secret to success: the journey really is the reward. And that isn't enough. It's the *story* of the journey, the *stories* of our journeys that we share, build, and experience together, and all that we make along the way, with tears and with laughter.

That is what Riley was born knowing, what Ed has never lost sight of, and what I believe we all have inside of us.

CHAPTER FIFTEEN

BACK ON THE ROAD AGAIN

"How does it drive?" I put the question to old friend and co-conspirator Taylor Perkins. We were in a large, mostly unused warehouse in York, Maine, admiring the old Willie Nelson band bus that a few years earlier had completed the Black Sheep's second tour.

Without missing a beat, Taylor replied, "Like a fucking *Tesla!*" Laughter ensued.

There she was, her brown-painted sides a bit frayed and tattered, but a work of public art and an invitation to something gleeful, creative, childlike. Every time I saw it, Willie's old tour bus rekindled that part of me that Pixar did: my innocent and playful inner child, my inner artist.

Stepping up her front stairs, moving just a bit past the driver's seat, I inhaled deeply through my nostrils. She smelled more musty than I remembered; she was one of the many bastions of community that had stagnated during pandemic isolation. Like so much of America and the world, it had been too idle, gathering no new stories and telling none of her old ones. With just me in her church-like, quiet cab, the question that I asked in my private monologue was this: if these half a dozen or so crushed-red-velvet chairs and benches in the front part of the bus could talk, what would they share? They might tell us where all the weed had been stored. Or which seat Willie preferred. Or where Paul English, Willie's best friend, drummer, and forcible enforcer, once stashed the cash earned at their shows.

A part of me was waking up: that innocent boy whom a second-grade teacher once scolded and reprimanded. That over-eager, impressionable young man whom Scott Collins told not to laugh at inappropriate times. That human in blue smocks, keeping company with other similarly-dressed humans watching Ferguson burn. This time, however, I was playing by different rules, a playbook that *we*, all of us Black Sheep, had created using many inspirations, including Ed Catmull's and Pixar's playbook for collaboration. She was our chariot for the adventurous mission ahead.

It was time to get back on the road again, to meet and celebrate all those unsung heroes reinventing the damn country from the bottom up. There was so much to do, so many new people to meet, and so many stories to tell, and tell differently.

The key to be understandable to yourself, to others, is to know and speak your story with love and confidence and support. This was a lesson of Detroit. That once-beaten-down city had a story to tell: us versus everyone else. But there was a bigger, better, more powerful story to start telling: us against the system.

I let myself sit. My right hand stretched right, touching velvet; my left hand stretched left, touching velvet.

Again: if only those seats could talk! They'd share stories from when Willie and Paul passed time (and joints) inside. It was a bus for manifesting destiny, a destination and a portal at once, most especially for countless musicians. Mavis Staples spent a couple of hours on the bus, just sharing stories with Taylor, while Florence + the Machine and Drake came aboard to toke up with their crews. Ray Benson from Asleep at the Wheel, meanwhile, still remembers when Toby Keith, just a kid, was running off and on the bus. Taylor always understood something unique about this mecca of creativity and humanity: from Dave Matthews to Snoop Dogg, everyone loved Willie—as a musician and as a human being who transcended genres.

It was hard to believe seven years had passed since we first met Taylor in Austin in 2015, back when he called the Texas capital home and ran a vintage-bus-rental company, one of the many companies he's birthed. From the start we'd zeroed in on Willie's bus, but that first year it was out of commission. That's when he rented us Barbara Mandrell's old Glitter Bus, as we christened it, back when Black Sheep was mostly just a dream. Back when we had no money, not even enough to put us up, so Taylor had even hosted a handful of us at his house the night before we pushed off. He was another one of those countless generous souls that welcomed us into their towns, homes, and lives across America.

Back in the warehouse, Taylor and his dad, Sonny Perkins, boarded the bus.

The day before, I pulled up to the bar at the newly renovated York Beach Surf Club, one of Taylor's latest ventures, a beachside motel steps from one of the best surf spots in Maine. Despite studying at Bowdoin College about an hour away, I hadn't known there *was* a surf spot, let alone a *best* surf spot in Maine. But my knowledge came from a reliable source in Sonny, who claimed that during the 1960s he became the state's first surfer. I watched as father and son repeated my own stutter-step on first entering the bus, a momentary pause, a slower pace, a deep inhale, and smiles arising with thoughts.

"We're gonna have to do something to get the smell of the weed back in here again," Sonny joked, as he walked to the back of the bus.

"That's what everybody always says!" I replied.

"That's the first thing that people . . . the smell of . . ." Sonny continued, his thoughts breaking up as he looked into various nooks and corners.

On the far-back wall of the bus was a photo of Jimmie Rogers, the father of country music. The original carved woodwork against the rear wall was a reminder of the craftsmanship throughout the bus. I watched Sonny running his hands over it.

"Whether you're parked in the parking lot of a school in the middle of the cornfields of Pennsylvania or out in front of an apartment building in Chicago, this bus brings people alive," I described. "It's just such a human space. Right?"

"Oh, yeah!" Sonny exclaimed, listening as he continued exploring.

"It brings out the kid in everyone," I continued, remembering the hundreds of people who had climbed aboard her on the last tour; even the intense, overachieving insecure suits melted into smiles.

"So you were involved with this?" Sonny asked.

"We took this bus on a cross-country tour," I replied.

"Who's we?"

"Um . . . uh . . . well, I'm the founder of this thing called Black Sheep, which has both a company and a foundation, and our foundation side took this on a bus tour around America in 2018."

"Aha."

"So it was an amazing vessel for our mission, which is to unleash creativity and bring people together. You know: try to build bridges."

"Oh. Yeah," he said. I wondered if I was reaching him, if I was making sense.

"We use art as the connective tissue."

"Oh. Yeah." Sonny still wondered.

"So this is an epic piece of public art," I followed.

"Ohhh, *wicked yeah!*" Sonny enthused, drawing his words out slowly and using a phrase that sounded as authentic from one of Maine's original surfers, another Black Sheep for sure. Just like that, I thought, this bus helps build bridges.

Pausing in the silence, I remembered all those hours gazing out the back windows, watching the ever-complex and undefinable country pass by. I never lost my optimism for the future, no matter how dark the headlines became, because the people we met, and humanity itself, always gave me hope.

Our mission with the bus was clear: it was a magic carpet for all those countless people around America who are willing to go against the grain, look hard at themselves and seek to heal their traumas, and create a better world every day. Those were our heroes: Aidan McAuley in St. Louis, the Fresh Prince of Detroit, or Nan Braun in Kokomo, Indiana, as she spearheaded a group of entrepreneurs working to reinvent her old industrial town. All the kids we met along the way: the next generation of Black Sheep.

A vivid recollection came to me of Danny meeting this young kid in a Walmart in a rural town, and how his eyes lit up and his smile widened to a big grin when Danny gave him a tour of the bus.

"This is my first time on a tour bus," Danny told the boy as they walked down the aisle, "so I'm still getting used to it myself."

The young boy we had met just a few years earlier had become a young man, and was starting to see the impact he could have on others as part of a larger story.

"I'm pretty sure one day you'll be here, just by the light in your eyes," Danny continued, as the young boy grinned. "And always be true to yourself. You're a cool kid."

A connection. A spark. Another Danny, perhaps, or any black sheep willing to walk into the system's discomforts, and choose to grow rather than become a victim or demonize others. That was our mission with the bus: it is *your* bus as much as our bus—at least if you are a black sheep at heart, which, if you've made it this far, I'm guessing that you are.

We all want to be understandable to ourselves and to others. We all seek means of connection, of trading a persona for a vulnerability for the chance of being seen as what we are: human. And art, no matter through paint or song, dance or story, and no matter polished or halting, seems the fastest, most universal way we do this. Except a very well thought-out and "incentivized" system has been built up around us to discourage us from taking any such risk. The system gets its legitimacy from quantifiable notions of success, and it expects us to make ourselves understandable to each other by adopting common scripts of success. In our culture, this is a zero-sum game of "I am more successful than you, and I have, earn, and deserve more sugar water and status than you." In place of our common humanity, we somehow strive to show off how uncommon we are, and the gulfs between us widen.

And just as in the movie *The Matrix*, this wasn't for *my* or *your* or *our* benefit, but for the benefit of the system.

This was the type of wisdom that my years of chasing the matrix's sugar water in the white-sheep world had prevented me from understanding, except for those rare, wondrous moments when Scott Burns and I ran into each other in the hallway, and just the act of seeing each other got us to behave briefly like two wild dogs ready to go play in the park.

We're all a part of a story, a much larger story than our tiny dramas and separate lives. If just we widen the aperture from own narrow camera shots, we can begin to see a story of *we* well beyond the narrow, system-organized story of *me*. Detroit, Aunt Liz and Uncle Joe, Ferguson, Harold, Nick: they all prove what is possible. The only way I learned to be a part of that larger story was to put my feet in the shoes of the other characters. Each in their own way had shined a light on the power arising from unleashing our inner child, our inner artist. And along with Aidan McAuley, Danny McGinnist Jr, Elyse Klaidman, Marlowe Stoudamire, and Kate and Phil Cooley, they were our heroes: creators, entrepreneurs, and builders of a new renaissance that is upon us.

As we open the aperture wider even, you see that we are all part of this much larger story, a story of *us*: the story of humanity collaborating with nature to make the most of this remarkable planet. Standing on the shoulders of our ancestors, each of us each day has the opportunity, in our own small yet meaningful ways, to grow into higher versions of ourselves, to create new lineages, build new bridges, and tell new and better stories.

It was time to get back out on the road again because we knew, as I hope you do by now, that this revolution will be improvised.

FAMILY ALBUM

ABOVE: Russell Industrial Center, Detroit

ABOVE: Harold O'Neal & Aidan McCauley, St. Louis, 2015

ABOVE: Beth Comstock, 2012

BELOW: Community festival welcoming
the Black Sheep in Greenville, South
Carolina, 2015

RIGHT: Mom
BELOW: Dad, Announcing the Dutch Flat 4th of July Parade, 1988

ABOVE: "Cowboy," our driver

LEFT: Alan Kaniarz at his shop at the Russell Industrial Center, Detroit, 2018

ABOVE: Uncle Joe

ABOVE: Phil Cooley, 2018

BELOW: Marlowe Stoudamire hosting us at the Detroit 67
exhibit he helped create, 2018

ABOVE: Tour bus group, 2018

ABOVE: Ed Catmull and Riley Sims, 2022

ABOVE: Rodeo Drive, 2023

ACKNOWLEDGMENTS

This book began during the isolation phase of the pandemic when I had the urge to write again. Exactly what, I did not know. Sitting in the small garden behind my house, noticing trees I didn't know I had or staring for hours at bees buzzing around, a soft voice inside urged me to express *something*. So I started writing short pieces, trying out a bunch of new styles, including writing in rhyme: about bees and trees, inequality and Jay-Z, and whatnot.

It wasn't like the Beatles going to India or anything, but it was fun to pick up a pen again.

What inspired me most was the prospect of telling a story about a group of heroic people few others seemed to listen to yet whose voices deserved to be heard. I then wrote that story, but my editors suggested that I become more of an active narrator. It was an approach that put me into the much less comfortable position of shifting from mostly observer to protagonist. The process took much longer than my prior books, and required a high degree of patience from the team.

I nearly put the project on the shelf after two years but publisher Piotr Juszkiewicz convinced me to keep at it. I want to also thank Emily Loose and Thomas LeBien, who provided large editorial support and contributions, as well as Tom Rath, who supported the project from start to finish. Paul Petters also provided great fact-checking support. Many people read drafts and shared helpful notes or comments, and I want to especially thank Chris Carosi, Suzanne and J. Crandall, David Duncan, David Epstein, Amanda Moon, Tom Martin, Farhoud Meybodi, Ravi Moorthy, Gigi Sims, Alexandra Wicksell, and Chris Yeh for their contributions.

Midway through the writing process, I learned that Detroit's Marlowe Stoudamire, aka "Ali" of the BLK SHP, passed away from complications after contracting COVID-19. It is not an exaggeration to say that Marlowe Stoudamire was a true pillar of the Detroit community. I hope that this book honors the integrity of many deserving people, including Marlowe, for their ethics, humanity, and hearts. These are the kinds of people whom we should be putting on pedestals: our true moral leaders.

Finally, Riley, I hope that when you are old enough to understand this book, aspects of your childhood, including some of the visitors to our house, will make a bit more sense. It's hard to imagine a "black lamb" bringing more joy into the world than you. Meanwhile, having dutifully honored my inner artist, I'll happily go back to mindlessly watching bees and trees.

ABOUT THE AUTHOR

P eter Eagle Sims is a best-selling author and the founder & CEO of Black Sheep (BLK SHP). After working as an investor in venture capital with Summit Partners in London, Sims became an accidental author, as the co-author of *True North*, the best-seller that has been selected as one of the top 25 leadership books of all-time. After that, he stumbled into Stanford's Institute of Design and learned product design and design thinking, an experience that helped Peter view himself as a creative for the first time, so he dedicated himself to writing his second book, *Little Bets*, for all those with untapped creativity. A top resource for innovators, it was selected as one of the six best advice books for entrepreneurs by the *Wall Street Journal*.

Sims has been an advisor at X, Google's semi-secret innovation laboratory. Previously, he co-founded FUSE corps and was part of the initial team of collaborators that started Giving Tuesday, the global philanthropic movement that raised roughly $10 billion in over 100 countries for social causes. He is a graduate of Bowdoin College and Stanford Business School. In all that he does, Peter feels most at home as a creative entrepreneur and innovator, contributing to making the world a bit more human.